Gentleman John

Roy Cavanagh MBE
& Carl Abbott

Copyright © 2018 Roy Cavanagh & Carl Abbott

All rights reserved.

ISBN: 9781723704604:

DEDICATION

This book is dedicated to the memory of Johnny Carey and all the players and staff of Manchester United in the post war years. They helped put the pride back in to a city ravaged by war.

CONTENTS

Acknowledgements
Authors' Note
Introduction   1

1. Crossing the Irish Sea   5
2. Six Lost Years   13
3. Let's Start All Over Again   22
4. Johnny's Going to Wembley   28
5. Footballer of the Year   42
6. Back Home at Old Trafford   50
7. Champions at Last   60
8. The End of an Era   67
9. A New Life at Blackburn Rovers   79
10. Taxi For…   89
11. Time in the Orient   96
12. So Nearly a Double   104
13. An Banisteoir   116
14. A Rover's Return   134
15. Gentleman John   138

Career Statistics   143
List of Figures   144
About the Authors   145

ACKNOWLEDGEMENTS

Roy and Carl would like to specially thank MICHAEL CAREY for all his support and help in producing this biography. We both hope the book has done justice to his father.

We are also deeply indebted to the following individuals who have provided us with so much help and support throughout the production of the book.

DAVE PRENTICE (Liverpool Echo)
ROB SAWYER
JOHN LUDDEN
LESLIE MILLMAN
(https://www.flickr.com/photos/manchesterunitedman1/)
NEILSON N KAUFMAN (Club historian - Leyton Orient)
RANDLE McMURPHY (Wythenshawe Red Paul)
BILLY SMITH (bluecorrespondent.co.uk)

BIBLIOGRAPY

The following books have been invaluable in researching this book:

'Winners and Champions'	ALEC SHARROCKS
'A Strange kind of Glory'	EAMON DUNPHY
'Manchester United, Forgotten Fixtures'	IAIN McCARTNEY
'A Tenth of a Goal from Glory'	PAUL HARRISON
'A Complete Post War History of Blackburn Rovers'	DEAN HAYES
'The Title'	SCOTT MURRAY
'Charlie Hurley'	MIKE METCALF
'Gaffers'	TREVOR KEANE
'Soccer at War 1939-45'	JACK ROLLINS

AUTHORS' NOTE

Between 1921 and 1950 there were two competing football administrations on the island of Ireland. The older of the two, the Irish Football Association (IFA) was formed in 1880 in Belfast. In 1921 the Football Association of Ireland (FAI) was established in Dublin. In a dispute that was not fully resolved until 1954, both the IFA and the FAI claimed the authority to administer football throughout the whole of Ireland. Until 1950 two international teams would play under the name of Ireland, the FAI team, that played in Dublin, and the IFA team, based in Belfast. Johnny and others would play for both sides until 1950. In 1954 the IFA team was officially named Northern Ireland. For the purposes of this book, the IFA side will be referred to as 'IFA Ireland', whereas for brevity, the FAI side will generally be referred to as 'Ireland'. More details of the history of the development of Irish football are provided on p117 of this book.

INTRODUCTION

I had the real honour of meeting Johnny Carey, the former Manchester United and Ireland captain, a man who just HAS to be included in a Manchester United team of greats. The most memorable meeting, although they were all full of his natural Irish lilt, was at his house on 15 February 1983, in the suburb of Manchester at Bramhall. The house, like the man himself, was full of its own charm and style, just as he displayed on the football pitch in his 17-year playing career.

I can remember the date as it was the same night Manchester United won their first leg Milk Cup semi-final away at Arsenal, and of course, was way before social media was around, indeed the game was not shown live on television, so Johnny and myself every so often switched the radio on to catch the score. In the end, United won 4-2 and the pair of us rejoiced in a fine victory.

Johnny was then in his mid-sixties, still looking fit, with a store of football memories which came over with the same ease that he displayed in taking Manchester United to both League and FA Cup triumphs, being made only the second man to be named 'Footballer of the Year' in 1949 (the year after Stanley Matthews) leading the Rest of Europe against Great Britain at Hampden Park in 1947 before a crowd of 135,000, and captaining both the Football Association of Ireland (FAI) and Irish Football Association (IFA) Ireland sides. He also had a very successful managerial career with Blackburn Rovers, Everton, Leyton Orient and Nottingham Forest, winning promotions with both Blackburn Rovers and Leyton Orient, taking Everton to their highest position for years and taking Nottingham Forest to the First Division runners up spot, whilst he also managed the Ireland team for over 12 years (including in World Cup qualifying matches), and coached the Ireland team in the 1948 Olympic Games staged in London.

The first thing that I noticed in his lovely house was the lack of anything suggesting that here was one of the games greats. The only sign was the actual Footballer of the Year statue he had won in 1949, so after a while, I prompted him by asking did he have any souvenirs from his glittering career. Off he went upstairs and came down with a large supermarket shopping bag from which he produced some very famous football shirts. The first was the white shirt of England, a plain white with just the red number seven on the back, worn by Stanley Matthews. Next was a red Wales international shirt with, inside a white square on its back, the number nine worn by centre-forward Trevor Ford. A green Ireland shirt reflected his many internationals, for teams either side of the Irish border. Then, a fading sky-blue shirt with laces criss-crossing where buttons would normally be, this was the Rest of Europe shirt from the 1947 match mentioned above. Finally, the match ball from the 1948 FA Cup Final when Johnny had captained Manchester United to beat

Blackpool had my eyes wide open, sadly again, this was not in the days of having immediate pictures on one's phones!

Over the evening, Johnny regaled me with stories of his career, from 1936 at St James Gate in Dublin, then besides his legendary Manchester United career, taking Blackburn Rovers up to the First Division his explosive ending at Everton, the miracle of taking Leyton Orient to the First Division and, him taking Nottingham Forest to runners up position behind his beloved Manchester United in the 1967 league championship title chase. He was a very proud Irishman; a great host and it was a proud moment for me to have spent time in his company. It is an evening I have never forgotten 35 years on.

Whilst these are my personal thoughts on Johnny Carey, perhaps the words of the respected journalist, Arthur Walmsley, printed in the Manchester United programme in 1965, give a complete view of Johnny's ability. Arthur was discussing the greatest Manchester United player in each position and his choice for right-back was Johnny.

Johnny Carey, a compound of shrewd soccer brain and foot craft, bringing an artistry in defence rarely seen then-or now. Johnny was not a full-back in the traditional mould of his day when the accent was largely on a robustness calculated to intimidate wingers and a big boot clearance that made no concessions to constructive soccer.

Johnny brought gentleness to the position-but it was a gentleness complimented by uncanny positional sense which spelled disaster for wingmen. But, having ground possession-in the best way was still to be seen of Carey.

Rarely was a ball wasted that could be passed to effect. He even indulged in the luxury and revolutionary tactic of the times of dribbling his way out of trouble so that he could use the ball rather than belt it!'

In an era now where anybody who plays a couple of years for a club is dubbed a legend, perhaps a new word needs inventing for a man who achieved everything in football. I really hope this book brings the career of a TRUE legend, a TRUE great of Manchester United and Ireland, the attention it deserves.

ROY CAVANAGH MBE
WORSLEY 2018.

The esteem in which Johnny Carey was held by Manchester United fans was brought home to me on the night that United played a friendly with Real Madrid in 1978, as part of their celebrations of their 100th anniversary. My father's favourite side was the team that he, and fans of his generation, referred to as the '48' side - the team that brought much needed post-war cheer back to Manchester with their 4-2 defeat of Blackpool in the 1948 FA Cup final. A team famous for its fast moving, flowing football, and the team that won Sir Matt Busby's first trophy. There were many United heroes that played in that team including names such as Rowley, Pearson, Aston, Cockburn, Mitten, all of whom had returned to professional football after the second world war. But, one man stood out above all the others - that man was their captain Johnny Carey. Prior to the anniversary game with Real Madrid, United players from through the years were introduced to the crowd. I was standing in the Stretford End that day and will never forget the warmth of the ovation given to Johnny Carey by the supporters in the main stand. To me, then aged 15, the '48' side was from a bygone age, a full 30 years ago. But for the older supporters in the main stand that day, Johnny was their hero, and there was no mistaking the warmth and respect of his reception. As I look back on that day in 2018, I realise it is now a full 40 years ago. In many ways, my favourite side is that of Tommy Docherty in the mid-70s. I can remember every match as though it was yesterday, and I will never forget the excitement of being a United fan in those days. The memory of the '48' side and Johnny Carey in particular, was just as fresh in the minds of those giving him that ovation on the night. United are a club with more than their fair share of legendary figures. There is no doubt in my mind, that Johnny Carey deserves to be considered alongside the very best of these. He has a significance beyond United too. He blazed the trail for Irish footballers – going on to captain his country and then become their first manager – a role he had considerable success at in club football too. Throughout all of this, he had the universal respect of teammates and opponents alike, fully deserving his title of Gentleman John. It is my privilege to work with Roy Cavanagh MBE to help tell his remarkable story.

CARL ABBOTT
BOLTON 2018

Chapter One

CROSSING THE IRISH SEA

JOHN JOSEPH CAREY, son of John and Sara Carey, was born in Dublin on 23 February 1919. Along with his brothers Luke and Danny, and sisters Sadie, Beda and Eileen, the Careys were brought up at 4 Adelaide Street, adjacent to Dublin's Dun Laoghaire harbour. The family were raised during a turbulent period of Ireland's history. Only 20 days previously, the leader of Sinn Fein, Eamon de Valera, had escaped from Lincoln Prison in England in a break out organised by Michael Collins. Collins and De Valera had both been involved in the 1916 Easter rising which was followed, in 1919, by the start of the two-year war of Independence. The political upheaval was taking place in a country of grinding poverty. Rural Ireland was severely underdeveloped, while Dublin itself, at the time a city of just 500,000 people, was full of notorious tenements. The political and economic situation perpetuated the Irish tradition of emigration that had seen roughly one in two people born in Ireland in the nineteenth century make the journey overseas. Johnny would be one more that made the journey – one of the many that brought so much to their newly adopted countries while remaining proud to be Irish.

Figure 1 Young Johnny

We will call him Johnny throughout this book. Though sometimes referred to as John in England or Jackie in Ireland, he was mostly known as Johnny throughout his illustrious career. That career started with his schoolboy footballing days, when the association version of football had to compete with the Gaelic version for his time. Johnny played Gaelic football with success around Dublin whilst attending the Christian Brothers School. He went on to play Gaelic football for Leinster College, winning the Dublin championships with them. Though Johnny also enjoyed association football, it was not the most popular sport in Ireland. Indeed, the Gaelic Athletic Association (GAA) viewed football as a non-Irish game, so much so that spectating or playing football was considered a disciplinary offence by the GAA until 1971. Given his early success at the game, Johnny might have been expected to pursue Gaelic football further. As it turned out, he would be denied the opportunity. Looking back at his career, Johnny recalled how he came to be banned from Gaelic football, pushing him to association football.

When I was about sixteen I had gone dancing on a Saturday night with a few friends, to what was termed 'An English Dance'. This turned out to be a big mistake for anybody wanting to be a Gaelic footballer as it was, apparently, a mild form of treason to flirt with the enemy like this. In my innocence, I did not know, but the rules of the Gaelic Athletic Association were inflexible. I was suspended, but what it did do was to turn me completely into a footballer. Although this puzzled and hurt at the time, I have not since regretted my 'indiscretion' in going to that 'English' dance and still consider myself a good Irishman.'

Johnny enjoyed many sports. When not playing football in the local Herbert Park, he enjoyed swimming and acted as a ball boy at the famous Fitzwilliam Tennis Club. Johnny believed these sports gave him skills that he would later use in his football career. Recalling how swimming taught him determination as a boy when he was entered for a 100-yard race which, as he had only ever swum 40 yards before, forced him to use every ounce of willpower to complete the event. At tennis, his role as a ball boy ensured Johnny kept complete attention on the game, again something Johnny would use to advantage in his footballing career. Tennis was also a sport that Johnny really enjoyed playing, and he loved seeing such as Fred Perry playing in some of the Fitzwilliam events.

In anticipation of a Free State, the Football Association of Ireland (FAI) was formed in 1921 with just eight teams. In 1928, Home Farm, a side formed as part of a street football league, playing their games on Griffith Avenue on the North side of Dublin, adopted the full name of Home Farm Football Club. Johnny started at Home Farm as a goalkeeper (a role which he would reprise on several notable occasions at Manchester United) before moving to the wing. He successfully played through the grades there, eventually helping Home Farm to win the Free State Minor Cup in 1936.

The quality of his performances soon brought Johnny to the attention of St James Gate FC who originally had played as the Guinness Brewery works side. It was at St James Gate where he started the 1936-37 football season, but he would not be at there for long, thanks to Louis Rocca. Rocca was a man who had been involved with Manchester United since their Newton Heath days. He was now the 'chief fixer' at the club and in charge of scouting. Johnny recalled how Rocca had come over to Ireland on the advice of Billy Behan, United's Irish scout, to see a player called Benny Gaughran from Bohemians. As it turned out, Gaughran signed for Glasgow Celtic the day Louis arrived! Fortunately, Behan persuaded Rocca to stay over until the Sunday and take in the St James Gate match against Cork to see Johnny play.

It did not take Rocca long to see that here was a player of real potential, as Johnny scored a goal in the first minute! Louis Rocca recalled the events after the match. *'I met the St James committee after the game, and they agreed to the transfer fee I proposed on behalf of Manchester United and then went home with Johnny to meet his father as I had to get his consent as Johnny was only 17 at the time. Mr Carey gave me a most warm Irish welcome that went on for a few hours! The following day Johnny came over to Manchester with me.'*

> ## Louis Rocca
>
> *Louis Rocca (senior) and his wife Mary, emigrated to England in the early 1870s settling initially in Ancoats, Manchester's Little Italy. They established an ice cream business in the Newton Heath district of Manchester.*
>
> *Louis Junior was born in 1882. He didn't want to work in the family business though. Instead, his one love was football and a team then known as Newton Heath. His involvement with the club began as a tea-boy at the age of 12. As he got older, he took on additional unpaid jobs, such as washing the strips and looking after the stadium. Louis remained a faithful servant of the club until his death in 1952.*
>
> *Although disputed, Rocca claimed throughout his life that it was he that suggested the name of 'Manchester United'. A decision which was taken at a crisis meeting of supporters of the club in 1902. What is beyond dispute though, is his immeasurable contribution to the club.*
>
> *Rocca became the chief 'fixer' for the club. Whatever needed doing he was the man to do it. To the extent that in 1931 he became assistant manager to Walter Crickmer. It was then that Rocca fixed another financial crisis by putting the club in touch with its financial saviour James Gibson.*
>
> *His two most important contributions to the club were still to come though. Rocca was appointed chief scout of the newly formed MUJACs (Manchester United Junior Athletic Club). The start of the famous youth policy that characterises the club to this day. It was Rocca that, impressed with a particular youngster's air of authority, brought Johnny Carey to United from Dublin.*
>
> *As the Second World War came to its end, United began the search for a new manager. Rocca told the club to 'leave it to him'. He knew the man he wanted and knew he had to act quickly. Liverpool were offering a certain Matt Busby their manager's job. Instead, thanks to Louis Rocca, it was at United that Busby began his management career. He started with a cohort of players almost all of which had been discovered by Rocca and United's scouting system. The rest, as they say, is history.*

Billy Behan only played one match for Manchester United, which was in goal against Bury in the old 2nd Division in 1933, but when he went back to his homeland in Ireland, he never forgot his link with the club. United, under the chairmanship of James Gibson, had in the mid-1930's realised that with money tight, they would have to develop their own players. First, a team of scouts were picked by Louis Rocca and club secretary Walter Crickmer. Billy Behan was asked to look over Ireland for United. Over many years, he would send some of the game's greatest players over to Manchester United.

That illustrious list includes Liam (Billy) Whelan, a man who had already won two league championships when he sadly died in the Munich air disaster of 1958. John Giles, one that got away, an FA Cup winner for Manchester United, who would go on to carve out an incredible career over the Pennines with Leeds United. He left Manchester following disagreements with Matt Busby as to which position he should play. Tony Dunne a world-class full-back who could play with ease at either right or left-back, winner of the FA Cup, league championships AND the European Cup with United. Kevin

Moran who seemed to always walk through brick walls in his United displays that brought him a cup winners medal, even if he became the first man to be sent off in an FA Cup Final to earn it. Alongside Kevin, another pearl that Billy Behan sent across the Irish Sea, was Paul McGrath. McGrath, an FA Cup winner at United, was a quite magnificent footballer. Like Giles, he would perhaps be better recognised after leaving United, playing for Aston Villa and most notably the Ireland side which Englishman Jack Charlton took to such heights. There were others Billy Behan would bring to United, but none would be better than the first man he sent over, having spotted him playing for St James Gate - JOHN JOSEPH CAREY.

Figure 2 Goalkeeper Billy Behan

Johnny, still only 17 and studying to be a Civil Servant, had only been with St James for a couple of months by November 1936, playing just six matches for them when Behan alerted United that he was a player for the future. This was a big chance for Johnny, with United offering him wages of £4-10-0d (£4.50) which was a fortune to him, as he was an amateur for St James. The exact fee paid to St James is unclear, with different reports putting the figure between £200 and £250. Whatever the precise number, it was a record fee for a League of Ireland side at the time. Rocca later stated that *'No greater Irish footballer crossed the Irish Sea to make a name in English football, and you can include players like Elisha Scott and Peter Doherty in that list.'*

The fact that football was the poor relation to Gaelic Sports, the relative poverty, and the Irish tradition of emigration to build a better life, meant that Irish footballers were an attractive proposition to scouts from English clubs looking for value for money. The record fee for Johnny should be contrasted with the English League record fee of that time which was £10,890 paid by Arsenal to Bolton Wanderers for David Jack. Jack had scored the first FA Cup Final goal at the new Wembley Stadium in 1923 when Bolton Wanderers had defeated West Ham United 2-0.

Though small in comparison, the fact that a record fee was paid for a 17-year-old with just two months of league experience speaks volumes about the potential of the young Johnny. As he arrived in a foggy Manchester on joining United, Johnny saw the newspaper boards proclaiming *'a big signing at Old Trafford'*. Naturally, he was feeling very proud until he read in the newspaper that the signing they were talking about was that of John Ernest Thompson from Blackburn Rovers for what was a large fee in those days of £4,500. Johnny's name appeared much further down in the same article, but there would be no doubt in the future who was going to make the more significant impact.

While it would be Central League football for him to start with, Johnny was joining a Manchester United determined to bring their own younger players through, with the signing of another young player, Jack Rowley a prolific goal-scoring centre-forward for £3,000 from Bournemouth a further sign of their ambitions. Sadly, United were relegated that season, but by September 1937 Johnny would be making his United debut, in the inside-left number ten shirt, against Southampton in a 2nd Division match at Old Trafford. The result was not what Johnny would have wanted, as Southampton recorded a 2-1 victory before a crowd of just over 22,000, but those lucky enough to be there witnessed the start of an incredible footballing career.

A newspaper report of the day recalled that Johnny was the only spark in a poor United display. The Manchester Guardian report felt *'it was a humiliating defeat and the long-suffering Old Trafford crowd was driven to vivid profanity. It was not just the defeat as the ineptitude of United's performance. The one bright spark was the play of inside-left Carey, a black-haired Irishman, who used the ball thoughtfully, and for forty minutes he played so well, it gave the impression United were actually winning. Carey at all events did not deserve to have so disheartening an introduction to the Football League.*

Figure 3 Black-haired Irishman.

Johnny did point out, however, in a newspaper article he wrote 12 years later that his teammate Gladwin was injured and left the field of play after 65 minutes, so Southampton scored their two goals against ten men as, of course, there were no substitutes in those days.

Another member of the United side that day was playing his last match for the club, Walter Winterbottom, a man who would go on to be the England national side's manager between 1946-1962. A further interesting note to this match was that the same John Ernest Thompson, the big money signing for United on the day Johnny appeared in town the previous November, also played his last match for the club.

The full line up for the debut of Johnny Carey, a man who would turn out to be a genuine Manchester United legend was; Breen, Griffiths, Roughton, Winterbottom, Brown, Gladwin, McKay, Bryant, Thompson, Carey and Manley who also scored the solitary United goal in this 2-1 defeat.

The Manchester United manager who gave Johnny his debut was Scott Duncan. A couple of months after this defeat Duncan resigned, going to

Ipswich Town as manager and then secretary after a certain Alf Ramsey took over the managerial duties. Ramsey and Duncan eventually took Ipswich to the First Division title in 1962. The ever loyal, reliable Walter Crickmer took on the manager's role at United in November 1937 until a new manager could be found. Despite the defeat to Southampton and the managerial changes, United would gain promotion back to the First Division at the end of the season.

Johnny would play 16 first team matches (along with 15 in the reserves) with Jack Rowley playing 25 and another youngster Stan Pearson, a very clever inside-forward, making 11 appearances. Johnny scored three times but his adaptability was starting to be noticed, as besides inside-left he would appear at full-back and wing-half. He still had areas to improve on of course, at times he seemed quite leggy, needing to grow in strength, but there would be no doubt that as Johnny moved further back in the side during his career from inside-forward towards full-back, the better he got.

Johnny's introduction into the Manchester United first team, especially at such a young age, was quickly noticed back home in Dublin by the Football Association of Ireland. Following their World Cup qualifying defeat in Oslo against Norway by 3-2 they decided to give youth a chance for the second-leg back in Dublin at Dalymount Park on the 7 November 1937. So, just two months after his league debut for United, Johnny was putting on the green shirt of Ireland in front of 25,000 with his first touch in that shirt putting the ball into the back of the Norway net, only for a linesman's flag to signal offside and prevent a dream start. Ireland drew this match 3-3, but would not qualify for the World Cup finals due to be played in Italy in 1938.

As mentioned, 1937 also saw the creation of the Manchester United Junior Athletic Club (MUJACs). With youngsters such as Johnny, Jack Rowley and Stan Pearson, already at the club more were soon recruited. Players such as Allenby Chilton, a very strong centre-half from the North East, John Aston who could play in many positions but especially either full-back role, Charlie Mitten a goal scoring flying left-winger and Johnny Morris who was a brilliant maverick of an inside-right, would also join United. Carey, Rowley and Pearson though, were now first-team regulars.

Johnny played his first FA Cup tie in January 1938 away at Barnsley which ended 2-2 as the result of a freak Barnsley goal, as Johnny recalled *'Whilst I scored one of United's goals, a Barnsley player scored directly from a throw-in! He hurled his throw into just under our bar, and Tommy Breen could only get a finger to it as it landed in our net! I never would see anything like it anywhere in my career. We won the replay but lost at Brentford in the 5th round.'*

After the English season had finished, Johnny went on a short tour of Eastern Europe with Ireland. A 2-2 draw against Czechoslovakia was quite acceptable, but a 6-0 hammering against Poland sent the team off for the summer with their tails between their legs! Pride was restored in September

1938 as Ireland beat Switzerland 4-0 at home before Johnny showed his scoring ability in his next two appearances for Ireland, a 3-2 revenge victory over Poland in Dublin in November 1938 and in another friendly match a 2-2 draw with Hungary at Cork in March 1939.

The Hungary match was memorable for Johnny as he explained *'It was great to play an international in Cork, and I appeared at inside-forward for Ireland. I recall we were 2-1 down close to the end and I was not having a particularly great match, thinking I need to do something to justify my selection here. I managed to get the ball just outside our penalty area and seemed to travel a long way without being tackled. As I saw their goal, I thought, here goes give it a bang and the ball fairly flew into the Hungarian goal! Whether it was myself or the Hungarian team who was most surprised, I don't know, but the Cork crowd went frantic with delight.'*

A return match against the Magyars was quickly played in May 1939 as Ireland embarked on another short European tour. The result in Budapest was the same, 2-2. Next, in a match that was played less than four months before the outbreak of the Second World War, Johnny would be in Germany, playing for Ireland in a 1-1 draw in Bremen.

During the 1938-39 season, Johnny would score six goals for Manchester United as he became a far more regular first-teamer, playing 32 times. He continued to show his adaptability, playing in defence and midfield but still mainly in the forward line. Indeed, his inside-forward displays drew comparisons with another Irishman playing across Manchester at Maine Road, Peter Doherty with comments such as *'he develops his attacks quickly and has a wonderful instinct for finding access for having a shot himself.'*

The last game of the 1938-9 season was against Liverpool at Old Trafford before a somewhat sparse crowd of just over 12,000 (played on the same day as local Rugby League side Salford lost in the Rugby Challenge Cup at Wembley Stadium). Those that were there saw a 2-0 United victory, with Johnny in the right-back position and a certain Matt Busby playing his last ever official Liverpool first team match at right-half. The report in the Manchester Guardian for the game played on the first Saturday of May 1939 was glowing about Matt Busby's ability, it commented;

'Hardly a Liverpool attack that mattered did not owe to its origins to one of those beautiful passes of Busby's, every one that seemed with strokes that belonged to cricket rather than to football- drives up the middle, square cuts to his right wing, mighty hooks and pulls to the left. Busby himself, the gentlest-mannered and most philosophic of footballers.'

Soon the names of Johnny Carey and Matt Busby would become inseparable…

By the start of the 1939-40 football season, Manchester United seemed in a position to make a serious title challenge. They had finished 14th on their return to the first division the previous season, and with younger players growing up together there was optimism around Old Trafford. Sadly, three games into the new season and the day after the side had played at Charlton Athletic, the start of the Second World War was declared as Adolf Hitler's Germany marched into Poland. Johnny, who had been born into conflict in his native Ireland in 1919 was now, 20 years later, faced with a global conflict living in his new home of Manchester.

The three matches United played in the 1939-40 season were a 4-0 victory over Grimsby Town at Old Trafford with Johnny amongst the scorers, and a couple of visits to London earning a 1-1 draw at Stamford Bridge against Chelsea, and then the final match before war was declared, at The Valley against Charlton Athletic.

That doyen of Manchester United reporters, Alf Clarke of the Manchester Evening Chronicle, (one of TWO Manchester Evening papers in those times, the Evening News and the Chronicle) always travelled with the team, covering them on a nightly basis for his evening paper and then in a Saturday night football special called The Pink. He recalled the eerie atmosphere in the capital:

'We had reached Euston Station on the Friday night. All street lighting was extinguished. Searchlights played around in the sky. Come the dawn, we went to Charlton, barrage balloons were flying around the massive stadium. The atmosphere was electric, but football was not the public fancy at that moment. If I remember rightly, about 5,000 turned up to see Charlton Athletic beat Manchester United 2-0 with Allenby Chilton making his United debut, but minds were far away fearing the future.'

Johnny had picked a knock up in the Chelsea match, so missed this last official football match at Charlton to be played for seven long years, while Allenby Chilton would have to wait seven years before his official debut as the three fixtures played in the 1939-40 season were deleted from official records. On the day after, Sunday 3 September 1939, the day the Second World War was declared, Johnny, being a devout Catholic who attended Mass every Sunday of his life, was in his local church listening to a sermon, when the preacher quietly said *'We're at war. God help us all.'*

For the record, Manchester United were in tenth position after those three matches at the point that League football was suspended and all results and appearances expunged from the official football record. It would not be until the 1946-47 season that League football would officially return. By then United would have a new manager to take over from the temporary custodian, their loyal secretary Walter Crickmer who had been filling in since Scott Duncan left in August 1937.

As an Irish citizen, Johnny had the opportunity to return home, as his native country remained neutral, but he decided that as he was now earning a living in England, he would adhere to their rules. As we will see in the next chapter, Johnny would continue to play wartime football, while making a full contribution to his adopted country through war work in Trafford Park, and then serving in the British Army.

Chapter Two

SIX LOST YEARS

Johnny Carey was just 20 at the start of the Second World War. He would be 27 before he could resume his professional football career. As soon as war was declared every aspect of life changed. Old Trafford became a military depot just two days later, as did United's training facilities at the Cliff, Lower Broughton. All but seven of United's 40 registered players were soon in the forces. The seven that remained (Johnny plus Breedon, Roughton, Warner, McKay, Smith & Bryant) were on essential war work. As an Irishman, Johnny had the option of returning home to Ireland which remained neutral throughout the war. Instead, though, Johnny adopted a highly principled position stating *'...a country that gives me my living is worth fighting for.'* Between 1939 and 1943 Johnny worked in the Trafford Park industrial complex at Metropolitan Vickers (known to those that worked there as Metrovicks). At the time Metrovicks was one of the largest, and most important, heavy engineering facilities in the world. During the war, the AVRO Manchester and Lancaster bombers were built there as well as engines and turbines for other planes. The importance of the work at Trafford Park to Britain's war effort would make the area a priority target for the Luftwaffe.

The work was hard, but Johnny still managed to keep in football practice, starting in quickly arranged friendlies and then the wartime Western Division of 23 teams formed in 1939-40 from widely differing opposition from local rivals such as Manchester City to New Brighton from the Third Division North. In October 1939, one of the early matches was against local rivals Manchester City, a game played in front of an Old Trafford crowd limited to 7,000. Johnny started in another new position for United, centre-half, in a game City won 3-2. The City team was an excellent side, including players such as Frank Swift; Sam Barkes; Alec Herd (father of future United star David) Peter Doherty; and the record scorer for City for many years, Eric Brook.

In a world full of worries, 0-0 draws were not what was wanted, and the games generally produced high scoring matches. Manchester United finished fourth in this season, scoring 74 goals in those 22 matches. Eight were scored against Port Vale, seven and six in the two games against Stockport County, six against Tranmere Rovers and, incredibly, both matches against New Brighton finished up 6-0 to the home sides!

At the season end in early May, a supplementary cup competition was arranged, with each tie being played over two legs. A 1-0 defeat to local rivals Manchester City was overturned with a 2-0 victory at Old Trafford before Blackburn Rovers knocked United out in the next round. Both sides lost their home fixture, with United winning at Ewood Park 2-1 before Rovers won

3-1 at Old Trafford. Johnny scored in both matches but was uncharacteristically sent off at Blackburn along with a Blackburn player after the referee felt they had taken their pushing and shoving too far.

Despite the deprivations of the war, life had to go on. During the summer of 1940, Johnny met a local girl called Margaret at a dance in Manchester. They seemed to hit it off from the start, although far from rich he had a job and was playing football for Manchester United. Margaret, incidentally, would always call him Jack. His mother, back in Dublin felt that he should return home, but Johnny was now 21 and most definitely saw his future in Manchester. Reflecting on that time Johnny's wife Margaret recalled:

'We were married at St John's Church Charlton-cum-hardy during the war in October 1940. Jack was working at Metro Vickers helping to make bombers while he waited for his call-up. His mother wanted him to go home to Dublin, but he preferred to stay. If it had been peacetime, we wouldn't have had the cheek to get married having only about £100 between us and no prospects, but being wartime, people did these things. I expected dreadful opposition from my parents and was flabbergasted when they seemed to be quite pleased to get rid of me. Actually, they thought the world of Jack. As time went on, they grew to love him dearly.'

Figure 4 The happy couple!

The future was to be with Margaret. With Johnny at Manchester United and Metrovicks, Margaret was working at the Prudential, alongside Harry Kershaw who would become the first Coronation Street scriptwriter. In 1941 she gave up her job to become a, full-time mother. It was a tough life as Margaret recounts:

'We lived in a furnished flat in Manchester, and Jack used to go to work on his bike at the crack of dawn in the black-out — it was a terrible life for him having been used to plenty of exercise and fresh air. At Metros, they worked all the hours God sent, and he looked deathly. We did manage to visit his home in Dublin for a few days, and his mother was very upset by his appearance — I tried to pass it off as the boat journey.'

Amidst all this, football continued. The Football League decided to alter the hasty format of the 1939-40 season and replaced the many regional divisions with one in the North and one in the South, both consisting of over thirty teams. The sides did not all play the same number of games, however. With so many players signing up for the forces, teams sometimes relied on guest players who would often be working in different parts of the country from the clubs that they were registered to. Johnny himself guested for several clubs during the war. As a result, it was a very easy-going competition with many complications over points won. The primary objective was to at least provide some form of entertaining football to keep the morale of the public up.

Manchester United would finish eighth in the league competition, while Johnny would score 12 goals in the matches United played that season, starting with a goal in the first match, a 3-1 win away at Rochdale. United's morale, however, was to be sorely tested by the Christmas of 1940. In December 1940 the harsh reality of war firmly hit Manchester and nearby Salford. The massive, sprawling munition factories of Trafford Park, with its many rail links and the Manchester Ship Canal, were natural targets for German bombers. During the raids, stray bombs hit both of the famous Old Trafford stadiums. On this occasion, the worst damage was to the home of Lancashire County Cricket Club. United's Old Trafford stadium also suffered, but only enough to cause the switch of the Christmas match with Stockport County to their Edgeley Park ground. Much more serious, of course, was the loss of over a thousand lives in the two cities of Manchester and Salford.

> **Wartime Football**
>
> *When Britain declared war on Germany on 3 September 1939, the government immediately imposed a ban on the assembly of crowds so marking the end of the Football League. All professional footballers had their contracts terminated. The total ban did not last for long though, as, on 14 September, football clubs were given permission to play friendly matches. The number of spectators allowed to watch these matches was initially limited to 8,000, later rising to 15,000.*
>
> *Between September 1939 and the end of the war, 784 footballers joined in the war effort. Notable examples include Wolverhampton Wanderers who contributed 91 men, Liverpool contributed 76 and Huddersfield Town 65. Eighty professional footballers were killed during the war, and many more were injured or became prisoners of war. Back in Britain, those that remained went into war work. West Bromwich Albion provided a striking example, when in 1940, one factory in Oldbury employed 18 West Bromwich Albion players.*
>
> *The first War Leagues had to comply with a 50-mile travel limit, and so the football association divided the teams into separate regional leagues. The first season of the Wartime League (1939–40), saw ten divisions established. The composition of the leagues continued to change throughout the war, in 1940–41, the leagues were reduced in numbers to just two: the North and South Regional Leagues. Crystal Palace were champions of the South and Preston North End the North. In 1941–42, the leagues were renamed League North, and League South and the London League was added. From 1942 to 1945 the three leagues were continued, now known as League North, League South and League West. The Wartime League's structure continued for one more season in 1945–1946 with just a League North and a League South. This season, however, marked the retirement of the Football League War Cup and the return of the FA Cup.*

A match against Blackburn Rovers at Edgeley Park starkly illustrates the vagaries that clubs had to contend with in wartime football. Blackburn Rovers only had seven players at the 2pm kick-off time. Appeals were made to the crowd offering the chance of a game for the visitors, and although it finished as a full 11-a-side match, the final score of 9-0 with Johnny scoring a couple of goals, showed the massive gulf on the day.

Just as Old Trafford was patched up sufficiently for games to be resumed, disaster struck again, only this time far, far more seriously. Germany's intention to blitz Britain into submission caused such a loss of life and devastation, with Old Trafford's football stadium suffering a devastating attack during a further bombing of the Trafford Park complex on Tuesday 11 March 1941. It would be eight years before United could return to their Old Trafford stadium.

In the last match at Old Trafford before the bombing, Johnny had scored his first hat-trick for Manchester United as they had defeated local side Bury 7-3, Jack Rowley also getting three goals. On the following Tuesday, Johnny had a first-hand view of the devastation that hit his footballing home as he told Roy Cavanagh in an interview in the early 1980's *'At that time I was working 12-hour shifts, 6am to 6pm at Metrovicks, although the management let me finish at midday if I was playing a match. After my shift that March time, I was cycling into Trafford Park and a huge ball of flame hovered over the Old Trafford ground and, obviously, things were not looking good for the old place. Fires from bombing raids were not unusual to me at that time as I had already been fire watching with Freddie Tilson, the Manchester City footballer, once a week over at Rusholme Public Library, sleeping overnight in case of raids.'*

Figure 5 The devastated main stand

Wednesday 12 March 1941 saw the Old Trafford football ground laying in ruins, with the main stand virtually destroyed. The main stand had been the administrative hub of Manchester United, housing as well, of course, all the players' boots and kit. In this moment of need, it was local rivals Manchester City who held out a very welcome hand, immediately offering United use of their Maine Road ground along with helping with kit and boots for the players.

Through it all football continued, although clubs were stretched more than ever as players had started to go to war and the general-public had so much more on their minds than sport. Johnny was, however, able to give the Manchester United supporters a cheer, as in the last match of the season they won the Lancashire Cup away at Burnley, with Johnny getting the only goal of the game. In the side were names that would become part of the Manchester United fabric: Jack Warner; Bert Whalley; Jack Rowley; Stan Pearson; Charlie Mitten; and, of course, a young Irishman who was already the toast of the red side of Manchester - Johnny Carey.

For the third year of wartime football in 1941-42, the authorities again tinkered with the format. This time, a Northern League competition would be played from August until the end of December, with a second competition, comprising some different clubs, running from January to May. Manchester United played well in both competitions, coming fourth in the first one and winning the second one.

The season started explosively for United, and Jack Rowley in particular in their adopted 'home over at Maine Road. They beat New Brighton 13-1 with 'Gunner' Jack as he was known scoring seven! Indeed, Jack was in sensational goalscoring form in the first competition, scoring four in successive games with Stockport County, four against Chester then five against Tranmere. Mind you, Johnny was in fine goalscoring form that season too, he contributed ten in the first competition, four of them coming against Wrexham in a 10-3 victory. In the second competition after Christmas, Johnny scored 14 helping United finish top of the table. Harry Catterick was another man that scored lots of goals for Manchester United that season. Catterick was the Everton centre-forward at the time but guested for United in quite a lot of matches, playing alongside Johnny. Twenty years or so later their paths would cross as managers in an extraordinary way...

During this 1941-42 season, Johnny also guested for other clubs, playing for Cardiff City, Manchester City (once each) and getting a few games in back home for Shamrock Rovers in Dublin. He would play for them occasionally through the war when he was in Dublin. During the war, Johnny also had games with Middlesbrough and both Merseyside clubs, Everton and Liverpool. The following season, 1942-43, would be the last time Johnny played a full season for a couple of years as he joined the British Army after he signed up for the Queens Royal Hussars. His wife Margaret felt this was a *'relief'* as the factory life was so hard. He played in the first competition until Christmas then would hardly be seen for Manchester United until well into the 1945-46 season.

Leaving his young son Michael, six months old at the time, must have been a particularly hard wrench, the lad would be four when his father returned permanently and initially found it difficult to realise who he was. During the time Johnny was abroad, particularly in Italy, he managed to get football practice in guesting for clubs. He quickly endeared himself to the Italian locals who christened him 'Cario'. He also made a big impression on the clubs he played for in Italy. There was even talk of whether he would go and play there, but Manchester was his home now, a caring wife Margaret and a young son Michael awaited him on his return.

During the wartime football years, Johnny played over 100 games for Manchester United, none of which would count in official records. Johnny signed off with a couple of goals against Bolton Wanderers on Christmas Day 1942 before taking up his British Army duties being based at Algiers in North Africa for a couple of years then to Trieste in Italy. His full wartime record reads as follows:

1939-40 P 20 G 5
1940-41 P 34 G 12
1941-42 P 35 G 24
1942-43 P 23 G 8
Total   P 112 G 49

MANCHESTER UNITED 1945-46

During the war, United Chairman James Gibson and Louis Rocca spent time looking at who would be the man to the club forward when hostilities finally ended. The chosen man was a former Scottish international called Matt Busby, who had been a mainstay for two of Manchester United's local rivals, Manchester City and Liverpool. Matt was also serving in the forces and would not be demobbed until October 1945, but eight months earlier on the 19th February 1945, Manchester United made one of their greatest ever signings when Matt Busby agreed to be their manager. While Matt was still in the forces, he came across a former West Bromwich Albion and Wales player. He was impressed with how this man handled players while coaching in Italy, and immediately saw the man he would want as his assistant. That man was Jimmy Murphy, who would become a vital part of the Manchester United fabric as Matt's right-hand man.

The 1945-46 season commenced at the end of August 1945 with two Regional Leagues and with no relegation. A full League programme finally recommenced at the start of the 1946-47 season, with the fixture list set for the 1939-40 season being replicated.

When Matt Busby was finally demobbed on 3 October 1945, he found his new side sixth from the bottom of the table. He was given an immediate boost, however, with the news that Johnny would be able to play in Busby's first game as manager of Manchester United. Johnny was on leave, as it would still be weeks before he was finally demobbed. Bolton Wanderers would be the first opponents for Matt Busby's 'new' Manchester United, and after going a goal behind, it would be Johnny, made captain for this game, who would score United's equaliser with outside-right Worrall getting the winner. Although Johnny should officially have returned to Italy the following week, he managed to get another match in under the new Busby reign. This time against Preston North End which provided an even more comfortable result for United, a 6-1 victory at Maine Road.

It was in the inside-right position that Johnny played in Matt Busby's first Manchester United match as manager, in which position he was a careful, technically sound player, who also chipped in with goals. Matt Busby would however very quickly notice that a better use for Johnny might be further back on the pitch with a switch to right-half quickly showing him in an even more cultured light.

Johnny finally returned permanently to Manchester at Christmas 1945 having finished his service in the British Army. His wife Margaret tells the story of his return *'At long last, the day came for Jack's return from overseas and Michael and I fixed a Union Jack out of the bedroom window which was the usual practice when a service-man returned from overseas. As soon as he saw it, he rushed upstairs to remove it as he thought it was awful'*.

While it was lovely to see his family, there would barely be time to relax as it would be straight into the United first-team for Johnny, scoring a goal against Sheffield United in a 3-2 defeat on Boxing Day, three years after his farewell goal against Bolton Wanderers during Christmas 1942. Sheffield United would actually win the Northern Regional League this season with Manchester United finishing in fourth position over the 42-game season.

The FA Cup was restored with Accrington Stanley providing the first opponents for United over two legs, as it had been decided the competition would be played. A 2-2 draw at Accrington was followed by a 5-1 United victory in the second leg at Maine Road. Preston North End would spoil any dreams of cup glory though, as after United had won 1-0 at Maine Road, Preston won the second leg 3-1 at Deepdale.

In March, Manchester United were asked by the authorities to help with morale for the forces still overseas, by playing a match in Hamburg against the British Army of the Rhine (B.A.O.R.). The game was uneventful really, although United lost 2-1, but getting home was the real story! After the match, with flying arrangements broken down, the Army authorities hustled to some effect so that United could be back in time for the league match at Bradford on Saturday. A special coach, generally reserved for high ranking officers (nothing less than Colonels), was put at their disposal on the rail trip to Calais. All the players had sleeping compartments. Imagine the surprise the brigadiers, major-generals had when the United players walked into the dining coach for breakfast! Johnny and Joe Walton shared a table with high staff officers from Field Marshall Montgomery's headquarters, with the other players also dining with various many starred big shots. The same sort of thing went on at subsequent meals, and by the time Calais was reached everybody was on good terms. Johnny was most notable for his easy-going manner, his quiet, effective humour, helping bridge the two parties and lifting the essential team spirit.

Later in the season, Johnny would move even deeper, into the right fullback position. Once again giving the impression that the further he went back on the field of play the better player he became. This was confirmed in the Manchester derby against City on 13 April 1946, a match which was a City home game, even though of course, both sides were now playing at Maine Road. The week before, the sides had played there as a United 'home' fixture with City winning 4-1, but this time it was a much different affair with United winning 3-1. Matt Busby had to make a few changes, one of which was the positional switch of Johnny going to right-back. He slotted in so well that he was to stay there for the rest of the season. Johnny could play everywhere, but perhaps now Johnny had found his best position...

Matt Busby had also quickly confirmed something that he had soon suspected, that Johnny had all the attributes to be the leader of his 'new' Manchester United side. It was not just on the field of play that Matt Busby was looking for leadership. He always wanted his captains to be ambassadors, show character and to use their intelligence. In turn, they also would have the, sometimes difficult, task of being the man going to the manager with the players' problems, which would mainly be about cash, and having to take back the managers answer, which would invariably be no more!

With the war over, the forces returned to Britain and football was again used to keep up morale and put a sense of normality back in place. International matches were arranged under the banner of 'Victory Internationals', played between the four Home Nations. IFA Ireland played Scotland in Belfast in February 1946 with over 50,000 present to see their locals defeated 3-2. Johnny was selected in the number nine shirt but played in the inside-left position. He was widely considered by those present to be the best player on the pitch.

Although not in the Scotland side, one of that country's finest wingers, Jimmy Delaney, became a rare United signing, as Matt Busby continued piecing together his team for the future. Later in the season, in early May, IFA Ireland played another match. This time in Cardiff against Wales winning 1-0 before a 45,000 crowd with Johnny playing at right-half for Ireland and Jack Warner, another United player, in the number four shirt for Wales.

Another two-legged cup match in the Regional League Cup against Bolton Wanderers ended in defeat at the semi-final stage in May 1946, but the signs that Manchester United would be a decent side for the return of the full league season in August 1946 were there for all to see. The captain of this emerging side would be the quietly spoken, versatile and much respected Johnny Carey.

Chapter Three

LET'S START ALL OVER AGAIN

The FA Cup recommenced in 1945-46, and the English Football League reconvened on 31 August 1946 in a Britain that faced the daunting task of post-war reconstruction. Many sections of the public had a strong desire for reform and change, and after a landslide Labour victory in July 1945, a radical programme of nationalisation and the establishment of the free National Health Service began. The desperate economic situation persisted though, so rationing and controls remained in place right through to June 1954. It was no wonder that post-war football was so popular, providing much-needed enjoyment for the masses.

World War Two, had also, of course, deprived many footballers of six of their prime seasons as players. The players too were understandably keen to resume their careers. Before returning to training though, Johnny was involved in two friendly internationals for Ireland in late June 1946 in the Iberian Peninsula against Portugal and Spain. The first game was played at Benfica's famous Stadium of Light before a 60,000 crowd who saw the home nation win 3-1. Moving across to Madrid the week after, Ireland recorded an excellent 1-0 victory. This meant a short summer break for Johnny, as a month after returning from Spain, Manchester United players reported for pre-season at the Manchester University sports ground in Fallowfield. Football was no different from any other section of society, and a shortage of any sort of training kit saw a whip round for clothing vouchers from the players and an appeal from Matt Busby in the press for the same.

The fixtures for 1946-47 were the same as those which had been arranged for the aborted 1939-40 season. The Manchester Guardian reported on the return of the Football League on 31 August 1946. The unseasonal, atrocious, weather conditions didn't put off the crowds:

> **VAST CROWDS WELCOME BACK "SOCCER**
> Arsenal Put to Rout at Wolverhampton : Bury Score Seven Times

Figure 6 Manchester Guardian Headline, 2 September 1946

'In spite of storms, torrential rain and the like, more than 950,000 people turned up on their favourite grounds. As was the case after the 1914-18 war people everywhere demanded sport excitement and they are willing to pay for it. Chelsea, with 61,264 provided the biggest gate of the afternoon, but five other clubs, Sunderland, Tottenham Hotspur, Wolverhampton Wanderers, Aston Villa and Everton all drew 50,000 or over. In the Third Division Hull City had a 25,000 gate, so did Notts County. At Swansea (32,000) and Millwall (39,187) gates had to be closed for safety.'

Grimsby Town provided the opposition for Manchester United's season opener. One significant change was that in 1939 the match was at Old Trafford, in 1946 it was at Maine Road due to the war-time devastation of the club's home stadium.

The team Matt Busby put out against Grimsby Town was as follows: Crompton; Carey (capt); McGlen; Warner; Chilton; Cockburn; Delaney; Hanlon; Rowley; Pearson and Mitten. They would, in the main, remain the line-up for most of the season, with such as Walton, Burke, Aston and Morris making their presence felt as the season progressed. John Aston was brought into the side first as a centre-forward before he got a chance at Christmas in the full-back spot he favoured. Johnny Morris would not be demobbed until the end of September. A crowd of just over 41,000 saw United beat Grimsby Town 2-1, thanks to goals from Jack Rowley and Charlie Mitten, to get the new Matt Busby era underway.

Jack Rowley had an explosive goal-scoring start, scoring in each of United's first five matches, all won, including an emphatic 5-0 victory over Liverpool at Maine Road, which must have been so satisfying for manager Matt Busby against the side he played for with such distinction pre-war. An interesting name in the Liverpool team was that of Bob Paisley, who would in time, become one of the game's most successful managers when in charge of Liverpool. That was the fourth game Jack Rowley had been amongst the goals, the fifth saw him get the only goal against Middlesbrough at Maine Road, a match that was witnessed by a bumper crowd of over 65,000.

The high crowds were starting to bring money into the game, and Liverpool reacted to their hammering at Maine Road by paying £13,000 for Newcastle United's centre-forward Albert Stubbins which raised an awful lot of eyebrows in the game. The figure being seen as a considerable amount of money to spend on one player in a game which depends so much on teamwork.

Johnny missed his first Manchester United match of the season when Arsenal visited Maine Road with another 60,000 plus crowd witnessing an emphatic 5-2 United victory to keep them top of the league. International fixtures were routinely scheduled alongside league fixtures at the time and the situation in Ireland further complicated matters. Johnny was unavailable as he was playing two internationals in the space of three days back home in Ireland! They were both against England, with Irish players still having the chance of playing for Ireland teams selected by rival administrations North and South of the border. The IFA and the FAI both still claimed jurisdiction over the whole of Ireland, and as a result, some of the same players were selected for teams under both administrations. So, on Saturday 28 September 1946, Johnny played for the IFA Ireland side at Windsor Park, Belfast. After a 15-minute delay to kick off due to the massive 57,000 crowd, this team suffered a heavy 7-2 defeat. Incredibly, just two days later on Monday, Johnny played for the (FAI) Ireland side at Dalymount Park, in his native Dublin. This match was a much closer affair, with England winning by a single Tom Finney goal to nil. England played an unchanged side over the two games with Johnny's Manchester United team-mate Henry Cockburn, making his England debut after only six matches for Manchester United, playing at left-half, and having a fantastic game, alongside the legendary Manchester City goalkeeper Frank Swift in the England goal. Another appearance for the IFA Ireland came along for Johnny in late November with a fixture away to Scotland, which sadly, hardly excited the crowd as it ended goalless!

Margaret Carey recalled her Jack's dislike of travelling by boat across the Irish Sea. Her comments also provide a reminder of the hardships facing everyone in Britain at the time – even professional sportsmen. *'Jack was always uneasy with boat travel although he did not want people to know it. In late 1946 Jack's mother was desperately ill back in Dublin, so we went over there. While his relations tried to feed us up, we just could not take it all after being used to so little as we were still in the rationing times back in England. I bought a pair of boots in Dublin which I wore to avoid paying duty- nearly everybody on the boat was wearing brand new boots although the weather was quite mild for the time of year. Sadly, shortly after we arrived home, Jack's mother died'. There was some good news for the family though in December 1946 when another son, Gerald, was born. 1946 was a boom year for babies- everybody having them it seemed as the men had come home from the war.'*

With Manchester United's continuing good league form keeping them in and around the leaders, the distraction of FA Cup football arrived. A visit to Second Division Bradford Park Avenue (The city of Bradford having two sides then with Bradford City as well as Park Avenue) was comfortably handled with a 3-0 victory. This brought a 'home' tie against another Second Division side, this time Nottingham Forest, but not to Old Trafford but to Maine Road. A large crowd of over 58,000 excitedly gathered to see United progress, but in one of the big cup upsets, they were to lose 2-0. Johnny captained Manchester United in both these ties, he would have a more significant impact 12 months on...

Johnny had a considerable influence on the Manchester United side of this era, so much so that whenever he was unavailable, it was felt greatly. None more so than in the return fixture with Arsenal at the beginning of February 1947 when United lost 6-2 at Highbury with Johnny absent due to an injury. He would also miss the following mid-week match against Stoke City at Maine Road, a 1-1 draw. Due to severe weather, this was an afternoon match, no floodlights of course in those days, and the game saw the lowest post-war crowd to watch a Manchester United home match of 8,456. The severe weather caused real problems for football with six weekends affected, prompting the authorities to extend the season initially until mid-May, with it eventually going on until early June.

The Maximum Wage

Post-war Britain faced a desperate economic situation. Indeed rationing continued until 1954. Professional footballers faced all the same privations of working people. Between the wars a maximum wage had been imposed which had been gradually reduced from £10 to £8 a week, and £7 a week in the close season. This remained the maximum wage when football recommenced after the war. For comparison, the average wage at the time was £4. In the post war years the maximum wage gradually increased to £14 (1951), £15 (1953), £17 (1957) and £20 (1958). These rises did not keep pace with inflation and the general rise in salaries. In 1945, the maximum wage was twice the average wage. By 1958, the average wage had risen to £15 and so a footballer earning the maximum of £20 a week earned just 33% more than the average wage. The players union argued that their members were worth much more and eventually under threat of strike action the Football League abolished the maximum wage. Johnny Haynes soon became the first £100 a week player. The system persisted informally though, and teams such as Manchester United and Liverpool set their own maximum wage of £50.

The Stoke match was an exception this season though for crowds. The footballers had been quick to see the finances flowing into the game and in February 1947 wanted their share of the ever-growing cake and threatened strike action. Football was a great boost to people's morale as Britain was going through a bleak time trying to recover from the war with rationing very much to the fore.

Continuing to switch between the two Irelands, Johnny captained the FAI Ireland to a 3-2 return victory over Spain in Dublin, his city of birth. In goal for Ireland, this day was Tommy Breen from Shamrock Rovers, also the man who was in Manchester United goal the day Johnny made his debut against Southampton in 1937. This match was in March 1947, a month later it was over in Belfast that Johnny played for IFA Ireland as they beat Wales 2-1 in a British Championship match. The Wales scorer was centre-forward Trevor Ford, and it was at this match that they swapped jerseys, the red jersey Johnny had shown Roy Cavanagh on his visit to Bramhall to meet him in the early 1980's.

By the month of May, the First Division Championship was really hotting up, and United's visit to Anfield on Saturday 3 May to play Liverpool promised to be a title decider. Johnny led the United team in a very tight match, with the only goal coming from Liverpool's big money signing Albert Stubbins, signed after their 5-0 hammering at Maine Road back in September. Stubbins made the difference with his goals for Liverpool this season and, in turn, became a cult hero of the Liverpool fans. So much so, that in the 1960's, Albert Stubbins would appear on the cover of the Beatles famous album *'Sgt Pepper's Lonely Hearts Club Band'* in 1967, Beatle Paul McCartney sending him an album with a note saying, *'Long may you bob and weave.'*

Incredibly, after the match at Liverpool, Johnny travelled overnight to Dublin to play for the Republic the very next day, in a return friendly with Portugal. Sadly, the Portuguese repeated their victory of the previous June, this time winning 2-0.

That 1-0 victory for Liverpool would be the difference at the end of the season which would not be until 12 June, with Liverpool beating United to the title by a single point, Liverpool had 57 points, Manchester United 56, beating Wolverhampton Wanders to second place on goal difference, with Stoke City in fourth on 55 points. For winning the title, Liverpool received £275 prize money, United's runners-up spot earning them £220.

Johnny would finish the season having played in 31 of the 42 League matches and in both FA Cup ties, no goals though, as he was now firmly the Manchester United right-back and captain. That role of captain was to be repeated the week after the Anfield defeat for Johnny when he received the marvellous honour of captaining the Rest of Europe side against Great Britain at Hampden Park, Glasgow. This was a celebration of the British Football Associations re-joining F.I.F.A. after a 20-year dispute. Johnny recalled how his invite came about.

'The Great Britain side was selected via competitions in the press with people voting for who they felt should be included. I was highly pleased to learn I was in a squad from which the side would be chosen, but it became clear that I would not be considered to be eligible to represent Great Britain due to being born in Ireland, but I could be considered for the Rest of Europe's side.'

By the end of March though, Manchester United received news that Johnny had been included in a squad of 15 players from across Europe, which had been reduced from an initial group of 50. A friendly was arranged over in Rotterdam against Holland before the eleven was selected. Johnny was then given even more good news as he explained.

'Before the match against Holland, which we won 2-1, I was absolutely amazed when the President of F.I.F.A came up to me and informed that I was not only to captain the team that day but also at Hampden Park in May! What a tremendous honour for Ireland, Manchester United and, of course, my family.'

The match was eagerly anticipated, being dubbed by the press as the *'Match of the Century'*. Fans had queued overnight for tickets for the game that was played at Hampden Park on Saturday 10th May 1947 with a massive crowd of over 135,000 bulging the famous old stadium to its limits. The two sides were Great Britain: Swift; Hardwick; Hughes; Macauley; Vernon; Burgess; Matthews; Mannion; Lawton; Steel and Liddell. The Rest of Europe lined up: Da Rui; Petersen; Steffen; Carey; Parola, Ludi; Lambrecht; Gren; Nordahi; Wilkes and Praest.

The difference between one team that had been thrown together, all excellent players but no time to become a team, and a side which particularly in the forward line was top class, was quickly shown as Great Britain led 4-1 at half-time. A stronger showing from Rest of Europe in the second-half kept the final score down to 6-1 but Great Britain player Ronnie Burgess was really impressed by the way, despite the language difficulties, that Johnny led his side by example showing wonderful skill. The massive crowd had seen the cream of footballers from across Europe. Britain, and England, in particular, were considered the masters of football, remember, this was six years before Hungary embarrassed England at both Wembley and Budapest, and eight years before the European Cup was devised.

Johnny had strong memories of the match. *'No international game has given me more satisfaction than this honour, and whilst the result went very much against us, there were many compensations. The Great Britain side was certainly a collection of footballers as good as anywhere in the world at that time, but I never found firmer friendships than those of the Rest of Europe colleagues with whom I spent many happy days. We went about our task just like any league side would have done. There were long discussions on team tactics, and whilst a fair few wanted to play the continental way of that time, which involved the wing-half's tackling the wingers, using the centre-half as an attacking unit and the full-backs marking the centre-forward we decided on the English style. Perhaps we chose wrong considering the final score! The social side was great though, I roomed with the reserve goalkeeper, Ove Jensen from Denmark, who brought masses of rations with him, butter, meat, cheeses, wow it made your mouth water! (Remember rationing was in force in Britain until 1954) We also practised penalty taking and I finished the best, but I was hoping we did not get one as I did not fancy trying to beat big Frank Swift in their goal.'*

Matt Busby finished his first official season as Manchester United manager in the runners-up spot while his reserve side managed by his right-hand man Jimmy Murphy won their Central League competition. Incidentally, the reserves were able to play at Old Trafford. Despite that success Jimmy believed that his team did not really have the players who could push the first 11 and both men redoubled their efforts to bring younger players, from all over Britain, to Manchester.

The first team though had performed excellently, and although they had the burden of six lost years, there was still mileage in those players as the following season would show.

Chapter Four

JOHNNY'S GOING TO WEMBLEY!

It had been 37 years since Manchester United had won a major honour, but 1948 was going to change all that, as United challenged strongly for both the League and the FA Cup.

The first four league matches set the season off like a house on fire, a decent 2-2 draw away at Middlesbrough was followed by two stunning victories over the previous season's champions Liverpool and FA Cup winners Charlton Athletic, both matches played at Maine Road. Liverpool were beaten 2-0, while Charlton were hammered 6-2, with Jack Rowley scoring four goals, both games being viewed by 52,000 plus crowds. When United went to Anfield and secured another 2-2 away draw things looked good for Manchester United. If they had gained the same result the last time, they had played Liverpool the previous May they would have been champions...

Then the wheels fell off!

It started with a close 2-1 defeat away to Arsenal that began a run of eight matches without a victory which only produced six goals for United. Three of them had been in a 3-4 home defeat to Grimsby Town. One of those eight matches was against Manchester City following their promotion back to the first division. City were able to welcome Manchester United to their home ground of Maine Road, with the United players having to turn into the away dressing rooms! A crowd of over 71,000 went home without seeing a goal from the two Manchester sides.

The tide of poor form turned once again when Aston Villa were beaten 2-0 at Maine Road. Manchester United then beginning a good run of form, going 14 matches without defeat, with resounding victories over Wolverhampton Wanderers away by 6-2, 4-0 away at Chelsea and 5-0 at home to Burnley. Jack Rowley was certainly amongst the goals this season, he had four against Charlton Athletic early in the campaign, and all four in the 4-4 draw at home against Huddersfield Town included in his 13 by Christmas. This change of form also saw Johnny Carey move back to the wing-half position due to injuries.

A midweek British Championship fixture between England and IFA Ireland took place at Goodison Park, home of Everton on bonfire day 5 November 1947 with Johnny again appearing for the Irish side who performed excellently to secure a 2-2 draw. Johnny was not captain for this match, Jack Vernon of West Bromwich Albion having the honour as the Irish faced an England forward line of Matthews, Mannion, Mortensen, Lawton and Finney! IFA Ireland themselves though had a marvellous forward in

Peter Doherty, and he scored one of their two goals.

Johnny had missed three games against Preston North End, Stoke City and Grimsby Town during United's bad run of form, but over the season he would play in 37 of the 42 league fixtures, scoring just the one goal against Derby County away. He also played in all the FA Cup ties, in what would be a historic season for Manchester United.

The much-awaited FA Cup draw would pair Manchester United away at Aston Villa, which looked a difficult match. Matt Busby had a different view, saying that he would rather play a team he knew all about as opposed to a Second Division side, apparently remembering the previous season's shock 2-0 home defeat to Nottingham Forest.

As mentioned, Johnny was not missing many games, but one he did miss just before Christmas 1947 was to prove significant for a young Manchester United reserve, wing-half John Anderson. On the day of the home match against Middlesbrough, Johnny felt that a stomach upset was so bad he would be unfit to play. Matt Busby had a quick decision to make because the reserve side was already en-route to their match at Newcastle United. He managed to get a message to Leeds Railway Station, where the reserve team were due to change for the trip to Newcastle, asking young wing-half John Anderson to return to Manchester. Middlesbrough had the excellent Wilf Mannion at inside-forward so young Anderson was in for a difficult debut, but one he came through with flying colours as United secured another victory, this time 2-1.

When Johnny was able to come back into the side, an injury to Joe Walton who had replaced him at full-back when Johnny had to move forward to right-half, meant Johnny went back to the number two shirt, and John Anderson stayed in the side at right-half. This enabled Matt Busby to keep a relatively settled team for the rest of the season. It would be the side that started the FA Cup away at Villa Park against Aston Villa before a crowd of over 58,000 on 10 January 1948: Crompton; Carey (capt); Aston; Anderson; Chilton; Cockburn; Delaney; Morris; Rowley; Pearson and Mitten. This turned out to be one of THE great games in Manchester United's rich history. Not just was this a memorable match in its own right, but it would kick-start a memorable FA Cup campaign.

Mind you it did not start off like that!

John Anderson who had kept his place recalled *'the clock in the Villa Park stadium said 2pm as Villa kicked off, it was still 2pm when we kicked off a goal down! Trevor Ford, the Villa centre-forward, passed the ball to his inside-left Brown who passed both Johnny Morris and myself before giving his outside-left Smith the chance of an inviting cross which he duly presented for the Villa outside-right Edwards to fire the ball past Jack Crompton 13 seconds into the match!'*

This Manchester United side, except for young John Anderson, was now a very mature team who just took this massive set back in their stride and blew Aston Villa away by half-time, scoring FIVE times! Four of the forwards scored, Delaney, Rowley, Pearson and two from Morris, while outside-left Charlie Mitten made three of them. Johnny recalled the mentality of that 1948 side; *'Villa scoring so quickly was probably the worst thing they could have done. We seemed to settle immediately, and some of the football we played in the first half was out of the world.'*

If the Manchester United team and the crowd thought this was over, Aston Villa had other ideas. Another quick goal at the start of the second-half was scored direct from a corner, although both goalkeeper Jack Crompton and Johnny tried desperately to stop it going in. Johnny was then involved in another Villa attack, with him and centre-half Allenby Chilton seeming to leave an inviting cross to each other, luckily only for Villa's Trevor Ford to miss a sitter that would have made the score 3-5.

That would be the score soon after though, and Manchester United certainly knew they were in for a tough match as the Villa crowd roared for more. With Chilton and Ford continuing their running battle, Chilton brought down the Villa centre-forward in the penalty area, so a penalty awarded, which Dorsett hammered home. With still ten minutes left there was now only a goal separating the sides. Fortunately for United, the steadying influence of Johnny as captain helped the team to calm the frantic atmosphere on and off the pitch, to finally seal the tie in the last couple of minutes with another goal from Stan Pearson. 6-4! Surely nothing could be harder if Wembley Stadium was reached for the final.

FORTUNE'S WHIRLIGIG AT VILLA PARK

By an Old International

Aston Villa 4, Manchester United 6

As all the world knew by six o'clock on Saturday night Manchester United beat Aston Villa in a thrilling, swaying, free-scoring struggle at Villa Park by six goals to four.

If Picasso and Matisse, jointly or severally, had been responsible for the design of this match they could not have given a more original twist to the proceedings. The Aston Villa forwards kicked off and in 13½ seconds were dancing back to the centre spot in delirious celebration of a goal which may become historic as a model of swiftness and surprise. Villa's opening move had been so perfect in design, so precise in execution, that not a single United player could touch the ball even; it was as though one of those theoretical blackboard diagrams, used by football managers to illustrate tactical talks, had really come to life. But the odd thing was that Manchester United were not in the least degree upset or ruffled by the game's ironic beginning. Calmly and blandly they set their own incomparable machinery in motion, seized and held the initiative, and by a beauty of method which seemed like a system of logic made visible they put on five delightful goals by half-time and reduced the Birmingham populace to a state of wide-eyed wonderment, if not utter stupor.

Naturally, with a score of five goals to one in their favour, and all going well, the Manchester portion of the great crowd of 58 000 chattered during the interval like thousands of red and white magpies. Fifteen minutes later they were as silent as Trappists, and ten times more scared. Within a minute of the restart a corner kick from Edwards dropped smack in the mud on the Manchester goal line and was deemed by the referee and about 55,000 others to be a perfectly good goal. Next, a thunderous free kick taken by Dorsett contrived, by weight and velocity, to bore a hole through a stout wall of defenders whence it rolled invitingly to Smith, who carefully steered it home. Five-three, if you please, and symptoms of unease, if not panic, developing in United's hard-pressed defence. Could anyone believe that at this juncture Chilton would give away a penalty? Penalty it was, most violently taken by Dorsett: and one can only congratulate Crompton on his skill in avoiding such a murderous missile.

At that most critical period, when the slightest slip would have meant an equaliser for Villa, if not more serious consequences, the calmness of Carey's judgment and character turned the scales. Coolly he faced and mastered all manner of difficult problems, trapped and worked the ball as easefully and confidently as in a practice game, and made it clear, by his example, that if United's younger players would keep their heads and play the football which has made them the talk of London, they would win. Carey's example prevailed. Back came the first-half brilliance and a great goal by Pearson in the closing minutes took the last fight out of Villa and sent long lines of sumptuous motor-coaches rolling buoyantly back to Manchester. Teams:

ASTON VILLA.—Jones; Potts, Parkes; Dorsett, Moss, Lowe, Edwards, Martin, Ford, Brown, Smith.

MANCHESTER UNITED.—Crompton; Carey, Aston; Anderson, Chilton, Cockburn; Delaney, Morris, Rowley, Pearson, Mitten.

Figure 7 Match report of a classic game.

January 1948 was to be a fantastic month for Manchester United. It had started on New Year's Day with a 5-0 home victory against high flying Burnley, followed by a 2-1 away win at FA Cup holders Charlton Athletic. The never to be forgotten 6-4 win at Villa Park preceded a home league match against top of the table Arsenal, which would see a record attendance that would remain the largest league crowd in England for the next 60 years, 82,950 bursting the seams at Maine Road.

The news that Manchester United had been given another 'home' draw in the 4th round of the FA Cup against champions Liverpool was tempered by the fact that as Manchester City had also been drawn at home, United would have to find another venue. Remember, this was 1948, and there was no staging of cup ties over three days because of the wishes of the multiple television channels!

Matt Busby took the bold step of taking his 'home' tie to Goodison Park, right to the home of Liverpool's fierce rivals Everton. In doing so demonstrating how confident he was of the maturity of his 1948 side, particularly after their thrilling victory against Aston Villa. Before that though, the titanic scrap with Arsenal in front of the record crowd had to be dealt with.

Figure 8 'Those far away places'

Roy Cavanagh interviewed Jack Rowley for another book many years ago when he lived quietly in Shaw, near Oldham. He vividly recalled the visit of Arsenal. *'A day or so before the game I went down with flu and didn't think I would manage to play. I really was feeling dreadful, my legs were all wobbly, my head banging, however, we had such a settled side, and it was a possible title decider even in January, so I had to literally drag myself out of bed on to the pitch. Arsenal were a great side in those days, managed by Tom Whittaker with players like Joe Mercer, Wally Barnes, Archie Macauley and, at centre-half marking me, big Leslie Compton, brother of Test cricketer Denis Compton, who was also on Arsenal books at that time. It did not help my flu when I saw the state of the Maine Road pitch, pouring with rain, it was ankle deep in mud! Still, seeing all those people trying to get in the ground as we arrived made me determined to play.*

When we started we were all over Arsenal, but their defence was in very strong form and, as so often happens, they broke away and after about twenty minutes scored from a corner with a goal from Reg Lewis. We continued being on top, hitting the bar, doing everything but score. When we did, it was a bit of a fluke. I hit this ball from outside the penalty area, and while it took a deflection off Compton, it flew into the net. We needed to win this match but could not get that vital goal, and it was Arsenal who were happier in the end.'

Johnny also had vivid memories of this match in front of a record-breaking crowd. *We were really grateful to Manchester City for allowing us to use Maine Road after Old Trafford was bombed and we were used to large crowds of 60,000, so, in a way you did not really notice it was such a significant crowd. Interestingly, they tell me that when they opened the gates at three-quarter time, more people came in than went out!'*

The mood around Manchester was one of high excitement as this marvellous Manchester United side had captured the attention of the public since football had returned in August 1946. Some 18 months on, attendances were huge wherever they played. There were 58,000 at Villa Park, nearly 83,000 at Maine Road, and when United arrived at Goodison Park for their 4th round FA Cup tie, thousands were locked out with well over 70,000 crammed inside the famous old stadium. Incredibly, remember this was 1948, the Manchester Evening News reported that an air charter company, flying small seating Rapides, was asking fans to pay four pence per mile for the trip from Ringway (as Manchester Airport was then known) to Speke Airport, Liverpool.

After a slow start during which Liverpool had chances, Manchester United suddenly hit the goal trail like they had at Villa Park, scoring three times before half-time. The second coming from an excellent free kick from Johnny which led to Johnny Morris hammering the ball home. Jack Rowley and Charlie Mitten scored the other two and Manchester United were firmly in control. Liverpool, with players such as Billy Liddell and Bob Paisley, just could not handle this United side.

The month of January 1948 ended with the first defeat for United in 16 matches and for over three months when Sheffield United beat them 2-1 at Bramall Lane. Though they had now hit top form, the league was out of reach, the FA Cup though seemed a definite target, and another 'home' draw, against Charlton Athletic, gave real hopes of final success. Problematically, Manchester City were still in the competition and had drawn Preston North End at home, so again, Manchester United needed another venue. This time it was over the border to Yorkshire and Leeds Road, the home of Huddersfield Town that would host the 5th round tie.

United had to make an enforced change due to John Anderson picking up an injury at Sheffield United, so the experienced Jack Warner came into the side for the FA Cup tie. Huddersfield Town's ground was able to hold crowds over 60,000 but terrible weather conditions on the day kept the crowd down to 33,000. Charlton Athletic had already lost twice to Manchester United, and they got off to a poor start scoring an own goal in the early minutes of the game. It seemed that Charlton goalkeeper Sam Bartram, was the only thing stopping United hitting a cricket score as he performed heroics. It would not be until the last five minutes that Charlie Mitten scored for United to make the game safe.

The sixth round of the FA Cup brought another home tie. This time, the game was able to be played at Maine Road, Manchester United's temporary home. Preston North End had beaten City in the 5th round, and it was they who would be United's visitors.

Expectations were high when the 6th round came around with over 74,000 packing into Maine Road. Preston had Tom Finney along with their very combative right-half Bill Shankly in their side. United had a returning player in John Anderson, although his return was clouded with sadness. John had been out with a knock, when his young wife tragically died after being diagnosed with TB, with the funeral taking place on the day before the 6th round tie. The decision as to whether he played was left to John Anderson, and he bravely decided to take his place for this much-anticipated cup tie.

Johnny was in majestic form, not only steadying his defensive colleagues but prompting the explosive attack. Manchester United took the lead with a Charlie Mitten goal and extended it soon after when Stan Pearson scored after smart play from Jack Rowley. Preston did get a goal back, just on half-time, but United were in no mood to let the chance of their first semi-final since 1926 go. Pearson got his second and United's third before Jack Rowley finished off a comfortable 4-1 victory over a very decent Preston side. Wembley was on people's minds as they exuberantly swayed and pushed their way out of a wet Maine Road.

The eagerly awaited semi-final draw paired Manchester United with either Derby County or Queens Park Rangers who had drawn 1-1 at Loftus Road. In the event, Derby easily won the replay 5-0, and the mouth-watering match was arranged for Sheffield Wednesday's Hillsborough stadium. United received an allocation of 19,500 tickets, which were heavily oversubscribed by their fervent fans.

Although Arsenal looked likely to end up as champions, United maintained their good form in the league as well as the FA Cup, until a defeat away at the always tricky Bolton Wanderers on Good Friday all but settled the title in Arsenal's favour.J

Johnny was a wonderful ambassador for Manchester United along, of course, for his native Ireland. His calm leadership style helped the team, who were now a very experienced set of players, letting their performances on the pitch be unaffected by the noises off it. This was tested in the run up to the semi-final. United stayed overnight in Buxton for the semi-final, and there was a happy, relaxed atmosphere on the coach as it made the relatively short journey to Sheffield. That was not the atmosphere though during the days before the tie. Rumours got back to the United players that the Derby County team were on substantial amounts to win the game, figures of £75 and even £100 a player were mooted. While those seemed way out of line, it was more than likely that Derby were being offered significantly more than their United counterparts. As Captain, Johnny was detailed by the team to ask Matt Busby to look at paying the players a substantial bonus. A firm NO was the reply Johnny had to take back to the dressing room. Matt Busby was an exceptional manager, his man management was first class, his own experience as a quality player helping him recognise most situations. One area he was inflexible on though, was about money. The wages and financial rules were clear, and he always adhered to them.

All that was forgotten as the game started at a cracking pace, which rarely slowed in the first-half, with most believing that the first goal would be vital. Stan Pearson was a great inside-forward, Johnny gave him the ultimate respect of saying he was the best player he ever played alongside. Hillsborough, 1948 was to be the day he cemented his place in United folklore by scoring a hat-trick.

Two of the goals came in the 15 minutes before half-time, although the Derby goalkeeper Wallace did not cover himself in glory with his attempts to save. Derby did get a goal back just on half-time which seemed to give them real hope, but the Manchester United defence, led by Johnny who was immaculate in his play, were determined that Derby were not going to score. When Stan Pearson completed his hat-trick ten minutes into the second-half, those Wembley Towers were now a reality for United who would be making their first ever visit to the stadium. The only time they had won the FA Cup was way back in 1909 at the Crystal Palace when they had beaten Bristol City 1-0. Having played FA Cup ties every two weeks from round three, Manchester United, and their Wembley opponents Blackpool were forced to wait six weeks before the dream all-Lancashire final would take place.

Blackpool had their own hat-trick hero from their semi-final victory over Tottenham Hotspur in Stan Mortensen. With Blackpool's other famous Stanley, Matthews, searching for his first major honour, Blackpool had a lot of the good wishes of neutrals. Another interesting fact is that in those days, League matches were played on the day of the final, and Manchester United had been due to play at Blackpool!

Johnny, like all his teammates, was inundated with ticket requests from long lost friends *'I received a sack load of requests for tickets, one from a friend who I knew from Dublin even said when you meet the King ask him about the Irish political situation!'* Johnny also felt the honour of captaining a side in the FA Cup Final. *'Players who have been fortunate, and I know that I have, to pick up a variety of honours in football, all agree about the thrill of leading out a side at Wembley will certainly be a red-letter day. Not from the notion of conceit, but because I am deeply conscious of the great privilege of leading out such a grand set of fellows as ours. We expect to be impressed by the vast arena and by the roaring crowd of multitudes, the ceremony, formal introductions, but once it is all and done with, I am hoping we can just give our best. That is all we want.'*

The FA Cup

The first FA Cup Final was contested by two amateur teams Wanderers and Royal Engineers at the Kennington Oval on 16 March 1872, with Wanderers winning 1–0. Subsequent finals were held at places such as Lillie Bridge, The Fallowfield Stadium in Manchester, Goodison Park and then the Crystal Palace. After the First World War finals were held at Stamford Bridge until Wembley Stadium became the home of the FA Cup final when opened in 1923. The 1948 final was the 20th Final to be held there. In modern times, the Cup has lost much of its lustre with managers focussing on Premier League position or qualification for European Competition in preference to a cup run. For most of the 20th century though, winning the FA Cup was equal in status with the league, and for fans, a trip to Wembley was the ultimate football experience.

Such was the interest in the FA Cup that the first Wembley final became known as the 'White Horse Final' after Billie a little white police horse helped clear the crowds from the pitch. The official attendance that day was 126,047. Fans found any way they could of getting into the ground with estimates of up to 300,000 being made of the actual number there that day. The capacity for the '48 final was limited to 100,000 and as always demand exceeded supply, particularly as out of a capacity of 100,000 the finalists each received just 20,000 tickets. Newspaper headlines on the day reveal the lengths people would go to for a ticket. Tickets priced at 7 shillings and sixpence (37.5p) were changing hands for £10. There were more ingenious methods for obtaining tickets. A Blackpool landlord offered a free week's holiday in his B&B for a ticket, and a Manchester woman even reported that she could get a house if she could find a ticket for her estate agent.

Newspapers reported the arrival of the Northern hordes in London. Many United fans were dressed in 'red and white suits and red and white berets with tassels'. Meanwhile, in Trafalgar Square, a stand-off was reported as 'Blackpool fans in pillbox hats perched on Nelson's Column and kept up a rattle barrage against Manchester fans chanting a war cry beneath Admiralty Arch.'

It is interesting to look back and see the differences in preparation for the 1948 FA Cup Final and how it would be now in 2018. Both Blackpool and Manchester United announced their sides on the Tuesday before the game, and it was Friday afternoon before United left for London. Although Blackpool had their two Stanleys as danger men, United were quietly confident that their overall side was the better one. A lovely late April Saturday greeted the teams as they moved out of the Wembley tunnel and onto that famous pitch, that noted journalist Geoffrey Green wrote, *'It was as if that smile of Johnny Carey's was shining over the whole world.'*

Manchester United in their changed blue shirts and white shorts and Blackpool in a changed white shirt and black shorts marched out of the

Figure 9 Leading the team out.

Wembley tunnel ready for action. These were the 22 players who would contest the 1948 FA Cup Final, Manchester United: Crompton; Carey (capt); Aston; Anderson; Chilton; Cockburn; Delaney; Morris; Rowley; Pearson and Mitten. Blackpool lined up: Robinson; Shimwell; Crosland; Johnston (capt); Hayward; Kelly; Matthews; Munro; Mortensen; Dick and Rickett.

Eventually, the waiting was over, and the final began. Blackpool were the quicker to settle, but United soon started having attacks of their own. Then, on 14 minutes, Blackpool struck. A lovely through ball from their captain, Harry Johnston, gave Stan Mortensen the chance to take on and beat Allenby Chilton and burst forward towards the United penalty area. While Chilton tried to recover, Johnny attempted to cover from his position at right-back, but it was Chilton who reached Mortensen first, sadly, just inside the 'D' on the edge of the penalty area, with Mortensen's momentum taking into the area as he fell. Shinwell duly converted the penalty. The reports the following day all felt it was just outside the penalty area and, should not have been given, but hey, this was light years away from V.A.R.!

Conceding the first goal in an FA Cup Final was not ideal for United, but they were not about to panic. Slowly they regained the initiative. Despite Mortensen still proving difficult to handle at the other end, both Charlie Mitten and Johnny Morris came close to equalising. On the half-hour United were level. Johnny played right-winger Jimmy Delaney into a promising position from which he whipped in a long cross. Although the Blackpool defenders seemed favourites for the ball, Jack Rowley had other ideas, he nipped in between them and exquisitely lobbed the ball over the Blackpool goalkeeper Robinson to bring the scores level. United were not to celebrate for long…

A Matthews' free-kick five minutes after Rowley's goal was headed on towards the United goal where the ever-dangerous Mortensen reacted quicker than any United defender and beat Crompton for Blackpool's second goal, and an interval lead. Indeed, but for an excellent save by Crompton on the stroke of half-time, it could have been even worse for United.

It was during the interval that as captain of Manchester United Johnny once again displayed his leadership qualities. He recalled, *'It was not my place or way to rant and rave, I just felt that if the team remembered just how good they were, relaxed and played to the best of their ability we still had a great chance of victory. It was vital we kept the ball moving and played our football.'* There were a lot of very strong individuals in that Manchester United team, Chilton, Cockburn, Morris, Rowley, Mitten, no shrinking violets there, but the calming, steady tone of their skipper had the desired effect..

The Blackpool left-winger Walter Rickett was giving Johnny plenty to think about, in what was perhaps his stiffest test all season, and with only 25 minutes left, even the experienced United captain was beginning to wonder how his side could change things. Luckily, United had their own version of the goal-scoring Mortensen in the form of Jack Rowley who repeated his feat of the first-half when he got on the end of a Johnny Morris free-kick to level the final at 2-2. All to play for!

The game was still end-to-end; first Mortensen would have scored his second goal but for another fine Crompton save, who then as quick as a flash, threw the ball to John Anderson, and the young wing-half's sharp pass quickly moved the ball to the other end, for the goal scoring hero of the semi-final, Stan Pearson to score a brilliant goal for United. Many older Manchester United supporters remembered shades of Harry Moger back in 1909, United's last FA Cup Final victory, who made a magnificent save at one end and quickly sent the ball at the other to settle the final.

Now the advantage was firmly United's and fittingly, with five minutes to go, their youngest player, John Anderson had the honour of sealing the FA Cup Final of 1948, only a month or so after his personal tragedy of losing his young wife. Soon, Johnny was climbing the many steps to the Royal Box to receive the cup from King George VI to seal United's first trophy for 37 years, and only the second FA Cup in their history. While recordings are around of the game a recently released one showed Johnny being asked straight after the match, cup in hand, what it felt like. He replied *'It is an honour to bring home the FA Cup 40 years after Manchester United had won it.'*

Figure 10 Proudly holding the cup.

As is the custom, the cup finalists had a function at a top London Hotel, in Manchester United's case the Connaught Rooms, but what was also the custom at the time was that Northern sides stayed over in London on the Sunday and did not return North until Monday.

In 1948, the FA Cup was still the highlight of the football season and after their victory players, officials and their families, spent the Sunday over in Brighton enjoying the sights and having lunch at the Hotel Metropole before coming back to their London hotel by coach.

Around Monday lunchtime the full party caught the train back to

Manchester, having one further duty before they met the waiting thousands in the city centre. That was to alight from their train at Wilmslow and visit one of the saviours of the Manchester United Football Club, Chairman James Gibson whose illness had prevented him from travelling to see what must have been the fulfilment of his dreams when he had come to the club's rescue so many years earlier. The players went into his room one by one, with the last being captain Johnny Carey with the coveted FA Cup.

A coach then took the team into Manchester with thousands starting to gather from Princess Road, culminating in huge numbers around Albert Square and the Manchester Town Hall. Roars of *'We want Carey'* showed the huge affection for this quietly spoken, pipe smoking, teetotaller from Dublin who had enchanted the Manchester public in general, and the United followers in particular. Johnny was told by Matt Busby after the Town Hall party that it was time to take the FA Cup home for the night and look after it. He duly did, by putting it under the bed for safety! In fact, the following morning he said to his eldest son Michael, *'Hey Mike come here and see what I have got'*, taking the young lad into his bedroom and saying, *'have a look at that box under the bed'*. When Michael pulled it out and looked in, there was the FA Cup!

Michael certainly knew who his father was now and had a brilliant relationship with him. He recalled Johnny turning his hand to different things *'Dad was always on the go-a great doer! He built three garages while we lived on Sark Road. We needed one for our car, but being such a nice guy, he convinced the neighbours that it would be a good idea - and would save them money, to build all three at the same time. He did all the work himself as well-the concrete foundations, all the brickwork etc.'*

Figure 11 Johnny the builder

The celebrations continued into Tuesday with lunch at Lewis's store in Piccadilly for all the Manchester United party of players and officials and then onto the Odeon cinema on Oxford Road where they were treated to their first view of the final via a Movietone film.

There followed the realisation that on Wednesday there was the postponed league match against Blackpool to be played at Bloomfield Road! A full house at Bloomfield Road of 33,000 certainly woke up the partying footballers, from both sides, and they put a lot of effort into what was a fine match. Stan Mortensen put Blackpool one up inside ten minutes and then tried to repeat the trick just before half-time, but this time he collided with Jack Crompton, the result being both players being carried off, no substitutes in those days. Charlie Mitten took over the goalies' jersey, and although Crompton returned in the second-half, no further goals were scored. Interestingly, Walter Rickett again gave Johnny as much trouble as any outside-left that season. Incredibly, there was still another match to play in the league, with United bringing the curtain down on their second successive runners-up spot by beating Blackburn Rovers at Maine Road 4-1. Further official celebrations were then accorded, Manchester, Salford and Eccles Town Halls all greeting the team with official lunches.

In is interesting to read Johnny's thoughts on the 1948 Manchester United side, and other footballers from the time: *'Playing with that 1948 side was an experience that never dims. I used to love watching our attack because I was standing behind them and saw what they were doing to opponents! All the five forwards were top class, but Stan Pearson was a marvellous player, a six-yard terrier we called him not flashy but deadly. I also, of course, came across other great players and great times. Playing for Manchester City in those days was a man I was proud to call a friend, the late Frank Swift. Frank, Jimmy Wilde the boxer and myself used to go round on sports panels organised by Capil Kirby, the journalist. Then there was a player I enjoyed playing against, Liverpool's Billy Liddell. Billy was much bigger than the normal winger, and we had some great tussles.'*

No	Name	Born	Joined	Debut	Born	Age Start of War	Age Restart League	Age Cup Final
1	Jack Crompton	Hulme	1945	1946	18/12/1921	17	24	26
2	Johnny Carey (c)	Dublin (Ireland)	1936	1937	23/02/1919	20	27	29
3	John Aston	Prestwich	1946	1946	03/09/1921	18	24	26
4	John Anderson	Salford	1938	1946	11/10/1921	17	24	26
5	Allenby Chilton	South Hylton	1938	1946	16/09/1918	20	27	29
6	Henry Cockburn	Ashton-U-Lyne	1945	1946	14/09/1921	17	24	26
7	Jimmy Delaney	Cleland (Scotland)	1946	1946	03/09/1914	25	31	33
8	Johnny Morris	Radcliffe	1941	1946	27/09/1923	15	22	24
9	Jack Rowley	Wolverhampton	1937	1937	07/10/1920	18	25	27
10	Stan Pearson	Salford	1936	1937	11/01/1919	20	27	29
11	Charlie Mitten	Rangoon (Burma)	1938	1946	17/01/1921	18	25	27
					Avg Ages	19	25	27

Figure 12 Playing record of United's '48' side

United's triumph in the 1948 FA Cup Final provided Sir Matt Busby with his first trophy. It was just-reward for his team which also finished second in the League, as they had done in the previous season and would go on to do the following season again. The '48' side was a much-loved United team, famous for its fast movement and passing style. The cup triumph and league positions though raise the question 'What might have been?' As Figure 12 shows, the average age of the side that won the cup was 27 years old. Usually, this would be the average age for a team at the peak of its power. Still with some good years to come, built on a core of hardened professionals each with 10 years or so of top-class experience. For Johnny and many of his teammates though, the war had deprived them of their peak years as professionals. Carey was 20 when the Football League was suspended in 1939 and 27 when it restarted in 1946. Six more of his teammates were on United's books before the war. Of these, Allenby Chilton, Jack Rowley and Stan Pearson were mainstays of the first-team at United before the war and were 27, 25 and 27 years old when their careers resumed. John Aston, John Anderson, Johnny Morris and Charlie Mitten were on United's books as professionals or juniors but were unable to make their professional debuts until after the war in the 1946-47 season. Of the remainder, Henry Cockburn and Jack Crompton joined the club during the war years. These six players, therefore, made late starts to their professional careers. Johnny Morris was the youngest, making his debut at 22 years old. Jack Crompton, John Aston, John Anderson and Henry Cockburn were all 24 when they started their professional career while Charlie Mitten was 25. Jimmy Delaney was the one exception, coming to United from Celtic after the war.

It is impossible to say what these players might have achieved if their careers had not been interrupted. It is hard to imagine though, that this team would not have achieved considerable success during the war years. In a sign of things to come, many of the players came into the club through United's new policy of nurturing young players through the MUJACS organisation. Had their careers followed an uninterrupted path it is entirely possible that the 1948 FA Cup triumph would have been one more trophy towards the end of a glittering run of success for Manchester United's first set of 'babes'.

After all this, at the end of the 1948 season, still, the football rolled on for Johnny. Matt Busby and United arranged an Irish homecoming for Johnny, both sides of the border, with three friendly matches, two in the South and one in Belfast. The team based themselves in Bray on the coast and relaxation was the order of the day. The games in Dublin brought big crowds to the matches against a Shelbourne Select XI and a Bohemians Select XI, which United won 4-3 and lost 1-2 respectively. The select sides included players from England, with three Blackpool players in the Bohemians XI. Another United victory followed in Belfast against Linfield with, again, a full-house appreciating seeing Manchester United's winning side, and their Irish leader Johnny Carey in particular, with him receiving a hero's welcome in all the three matches.

Johnny repaid some of the affection by leading Ireland's international side as they again visited Spain and Portugal in late May 1948 with large crowds of 65,000 at the Olympic Stadium in Barcelona seeing Spain gain revenge for two recent defeats, winning 2-1 and over 50,000 in Lisbon as Portugal again had the upper hand over the Irish, winning 2-0.

Finally, though, Johnny was able to relax and enjoy some time with his family after a momentous year. He could go off with the new song that the Manchester United fans had created called 'The Irish Lad.'

Hello, Johnny Carey you can hear the girls all cry.
Hello, Johnny Carey, you're the apple of my eye.
You're a decent boy from Ireland there is no one can deny.
You're a harem scarum devil may careum decent Irish boy'.

Chapter Five

FOOTBALLER OF THE YEAR

By the start of the 1948-49 season, Johnny Carey was 29, and although still very fit and successful, opportunities for the future had to be explored. One such opportunity came around in late July 1948 when Ireland asked him to coach their Olympic football team in the London Olympics of that year.

Ireland had first competed at football in the 1924 Paris Olympics. Following the three-year Irish War of Independence, the football authorities entered a side which beat Belgium 1-0 in the 1st round before losing in a 2-1 extra-time defeat to the Netherlands. Twenty-four years later, the same two nations, would be drawn to play a preliminary round match staged at Portsmouth's Fratton Park with Johnny taking charge of the Irish team. A crowd of 8,000 watched the Netherlands win 3-1, incidentally going on to play the Great Britain team managed by Matt Busby at Arsenal's Highbury Stadium. That match would go into extra-time with Great Britain winning 4-3, eventually losing in the semi-finals 3-1 to Yugoslavia. Yugoslavia went on to lose the final to Sweden by the same score.

Though all too brief, that first taste of coaching and leading a football team would benefit Johnny's career a few years later, but back in 1948, he was ready for the start of the new season with Manchester United. Having finished runners-up in the previous two seasons, United were determined to go one better in the 1948-49 season. Losing the opening match of the season 2-1 at home to Derby County was not the start Johnny and his team wanted. Johnny, though, would go on to have another memorable season, becoming the second recipient of the new Footballer of The Year award, following Stanley Matthews the previous year. He would also have a tremendously consistent appearance record, missing just one of Manchester United's 42 league matches (playing an international the same day) and appearing in seven of their eight cup ties.

After the Derby County disappointment, a couple of impressive away victories, 3-0 at Blackpool and 1-0 at champions Arsenal, offered reassurance to their supporters, but it was a very mixed bag of results. Blackpool, for instance, coming to Maine Road and winning 4-3, before the first chance of another trophy for Johnny and his team appeared in the form of the Charity Shield.

Manchester United play a prominent role in the history of the Charity Shield. They took part in the very first match, which is still the only one ever to go to a replay, a 1-1 draw against Queens Park Rangers in 1908 with the replay resulting in a 4-0 United victory. Then, in 1911, Manchester United recorded the largest ever score in the competition, an 8-4 win over Swindon Town. In those days the Charity Shield wasn't the 'traditional curtain raiser'

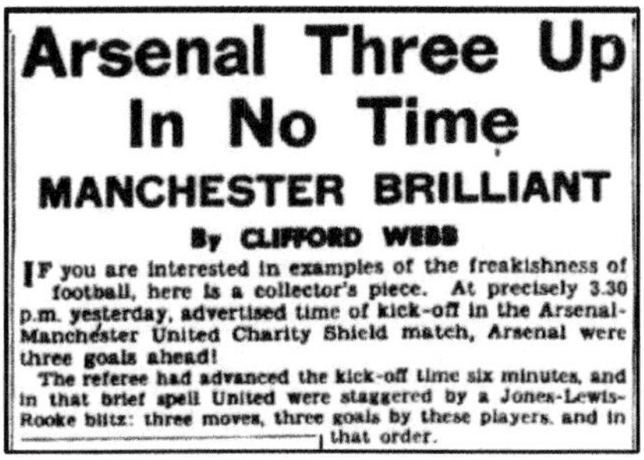

Arsenal Three Up In No Time
MANCHESTER BRILLIANT
By CLIFFORD WEBB

IF you are interested in examples of the freakishness of football, here is a collector's piece. At precisely 3.30 p.m. yesterday, advertised time of kick-off in the Arsenal-Manchester United Charity Shield match, Arsenal were three goals ahead!

The referee had advanced the kick-off time six minutes, and in that brief spell United were staggered by a Jones-Lewis-Rooke blitz: three moves, three goals by these players, and in that order.

Figure 13 'Arsenal Three Up'

that we are now used to., and it was in early October 1948 that United travelled to Highbury with optimism to play Arsenal, particularly as they had already defeated the defending champions 1-0 at Highbury in the third match of the season. Arsenal made an explosive start to the game though. So much so, that they were three up before the official kick-off time after the referee decided to start the game six minutes early! Arsenal scored those three goals in a five-minute spell and led 4-2 at half-time. An own goal by Arsenal gave United renewed hope, and they dominated the last 20 minutes but were unable to equalise.

The only league fixture Johnny missed this season came on the Saturday after the mid-week Charity Shield match, as he captained IFA Ireland against England in the British Championship match in Belfast. He would face teammates Henry Cockburn and Stan Pearson, and it was they who celebrated, as England scored an emphatic 6-2 victory with Stan Mortensen scoring a hat-trick.

On his return to the United side, Johnny was able to help revitalise his team as they went on a 13-match unbeaten run in the league that would eventually lead to a third consecutive runners-up spot in the league. In the FA Cup, as defending champions, Manchester United made a real fist of retaining the trophy, drawing huge attendances on the way to an eventual semi-final replay defeat at the hands of Wolverhampton Wanderers.

Before the FA Cup started though, Johnny continued to play for both of the two Irish football federations. The first game was another British Championship fixture for the IFA Ireland team, a match at Glasgow against Scotland which drew an incredible crowd of 93,000 for a mid-week international. A couple of weeks later, it was over to Dublin to captain FAI Ireland in their friendly with Switzerland, with the crowd of 25,000 left disappointed by a 1-0 defeat.

There was also another arrival at the Carey household as Johnny and Margaret already having two sons, decided that they would adopt a girl and three years after the birth of Gerald they adopted a bonny girl called Marie.

AMAZING CUP ATTENDANCES

As FA Cup holders, Manchester United were determined to keep their trophy, with the Manchester public also determined to give their support. The 3rd round draw produced a home tie against Bournemouth & Boscombe from the Third Division South to be played at Maine Road. A crowd of 55,000 was the first of a series of immense crowds that would watch United over the next six weeks as they progressed to the 6th round of the FA Cup.

Bournemouth were comfortably dispatched 6-0, and another Third Division side awaited in the 4th round, this time from the North section, Bradford Park Avenue. It is still hard to believe, 70 years on, that the second largest home crowd in Manchester United's history, 82,771 would be drawn to such a seemingly one-sided match-up. Nothing, however, is inevitable in football, particularly cup football, as Bradford Park Avenue showed by taking a first-half lead. A Charlie Mitten equaliser in the second-half took the tie to extra-time but still no further goals. Extra-time was played at the time, as mid-week matches were thought to reduce the productivity urgently needed as Britain tried to rebuild after the war.

The replay was arranged for the following Saturday at the famous old Park Avenue stadium at Bradford, another of the twenty or so football stadiums designed by Archibald Leitch across Britain. A full house of 30,000 fully expected this time, that Johnny and his cup holders would finish off the local heroes, but an icy pitch and fog swirling around made abilities more equal. The draw for the 5th round decreed that the winners would be paired with non-league Yeovil Town, so Bradford Park Avenue also saw a route to the 6th round. Yet another 1-1 draw, again after extra time, meant the sides had played 240 minutes without breaking the deadlock between the FA Cup holders and a Third Division North team.

This time, a mid-week replay was necessary with the date quickly set for the Monday afternoon back in Manchester. Officially just over 70,000 was recorded as the official attendance, but thousands climbed over walls or forced their way over turnstiles, obviously relishing the chance to get off work, productivity or not! Finally, Manchester United turned on their style and won 5-0, to bring non-league Yeovil Town to Maine Road the following Saturday.

When over 81,000 turned up for the Yeovil tie, it meant that inside six weeks, around 320,000 people had watched Manchester United play five FA Cup matches, a fact not lost on footballers on tight maximum wages. Following their return to goalscoring form the previous Monday, United's forwards had a taste for more, particularly Jack Rowley, who scored five times, including a hat-trick inside 15 minutes, as United ended Yeovil's cup dreams 8-0.

The luck of the draw is always handy in cup competitions, and after the previous season when Manchester United had drawn first division sides in every round when winning the FA Cup, this season had already brought a non-league side and two Third Division sides, when they were paired with another minnow, being drawn away at Hull City of the Third Division North. Johnny would miss his only game of the season for the Hull tie, as when he missed his only league fixture he was playing an international that day for IFA Ireland. Another full house at Boothferry Park Hull, over 55,000 a club record, saw United really stretched, but another visit to Wembley was undoubtedly in the sights of the players, and they won a hard-fought match 1-0.

The semi-final draw paired Manchester United with Wolverhampton Wanderers at Hillsborough, site of the previous season's victory over Derby County at the same stage. Before the semi-final took place, United were rocked by the transfer of Johnny Morris to Derby County. The background went back to the pre-season when the simmering frustrations of a lot of the players over money had come to the surface. Rumours of other teams receiving payments for success did not go down well, and of course, the close season had seen the wages reduced, as per the then rules of the game. But, following the club's post-war success and the attention the club received being reflected in the large crowds that they attracted, a resentment brewed among the players and Johnny was asked to approach Matt Busby for a meeting.

Pre-season, Johnny had rejected his teammates' request. This hardened the attitude of the remaining moderates towards that of the more outspoken players such as Johnny Morris, Charlie Mitten and Henry Cockburn. The team as one shouted Johnny down and insisted on him seeing Matt Busby. He pointed out the rules of the Football League and, as a man of real principle that would be it. A request for new golf clubs to be given to the players was ignored and the team's performance in the opening game of the season at home to Derby County perhaps reflected the depth of frustration in so many of them. A solution to new golf clubs issue was arranged early in the season, and the team were soon up and around the front-runners, and of course, making great strides in their FA Cup defence.

Johnny Morris though, despite being a very fine inside-right always had a definite idea of how players should be treated. His working relationship with Matt Busby was undoubtedly on edge, and when he was not restored immediately to the side after recovering from an injury, things came to a head. A couple of incidents in training left Matt Busby feeling he had to take a stand. Johnny Morris did not believe he would do anything, but Busby did and alerted the press that Morris wanted away and before Johnny Morris knew, a deal with Derby County was sorted.

Coming just before an important FA Cup Semi-Final this was a courageous decision on Busby's part, which his captain Johnny felt was the correct one. He was close to his manager, and the way that the great man dealt with all these incidents would be stored by Johnny for when he would take the step into management. Johnny certainly had many of the attributes of Matt Busby, always smart in his dress sense, a natural leader, a reasoned, cool well-mannered man, a man of the Catholic faith whose values he held firm. Johnny was also teetotal and a non-cigarette smoker, although rarely seen without his pipe!

> **THREAT TO IRISH PLAYERS**
>
> *Police to Take Extra Precautions*
>
> EXTRA police precautions will be taken as a result of threats to players engaged in to-day's match between Ireland and Wales at Windsor Park, Belfast, home of the Linfield Club.
>
> Anonymous letters were received at week-end by Manchester United and West Bromwich Albion threatening assault on Carey, Vernon and Walsh.
>
> The letters said that if the clubs persisted in allowing "these Fenian players" to take part in the game "we will make a worse mess of them than we did to Jimmy Jones."

Figure 14 Threat to Irish Players (Aberdeen Press)

Before the semi-final, Johnny was to make the last of his nine appearances for the Belfast based IFA Ireland team. The match was played as part of the 1948-49 British Championship which also doubled as a qualifier for the forthcoming 1950 World Cup Finals. Result wise, it was not a happy ending as Wales won 2-0 leaving IFA Ireland bottom of the Home Nations and not going to Brazil for the World Cup. Johnny, however, would be given another chance to qualify for the World Cup later in 1949 via the Dublin based FAI selected Ireland's qualifying group. The anomaly of players being able to represent two rival versions of Ireland could not continue indefinitely and there was increasing pressure placed on players that continued to represent both Irelands, backed by a campaign led by the chairman of Shamrock Rovers. Eventually, in April 1950 Johnny would confirm that he was no longer available for selection by the IFA, committing himself to the Dublin based FAI.

Johnny then reverted his attention back to helping United qualify for the 1949 FA Cup Final at the semi-final against Wolverhampton Wanderers at Hillsborough. A full house of 62,000 was eager to see how United would fare after the shock transfer of Johnny Morris. The team Manchester United put out for the match saw both positional and personnel changes from the previous season's final. John Anderson was pushed into Morris's number eight shirt with Henry Cockburn switching from left to right-half and Billy McGlen taking his number six shirt.

The match with Wolverhampton Wanderers was very physical, which was out of character as both teams were renowned as 'footballing' sides. Both full-backs for Wolverhampton suffered early injuries, while both Jack Rowley and Henry Cockburn suffered head injuries for United. Each side scored in the first-half, both goals from mistakes, and although United were clearly on top in the second-half, they could not get the winner. It meant a replay which was moved to Everton's Goodison Park. Before that, Johnny received a marvellous award...

FOOTBALLER OF THE YEAR

To give it its full title, The Football Writers Association Footballer of the Year Award was first made in 1948 when Stanley Matthews of Blackpool was the inaugural recipient. In 1949 the award was given to Johnny Carey and was announced between the semi-final match and replay between United and

Wolverhampton Wanderers. Johnny polled 40% of the votes with the next two players Billy Wright and Raich Carter only getting that number together. It was a fitting tribute to a man who held himself to the highest standards and was respected by all as an excellent player and a fine man. On the day Johnny heard the news he went to the Ardwick Hippodrome, close to Piccadilly in Manchester, to attend an event with his wife Margaret and his friend the famous broadcaster Eamonn Andrews, with everybody congratulating him on his marvellous achievement. The award was presented to Johnny in London at the Football Writers Dinner, where Johnny was accompanied by his manager Matt Busby. This dinner became associated with the evening before the FA Cup Final, sadly, 1949 would not see Manchester United playing at Wembley the following day.

The semi-final replay against Wolverhampton Wanderers had continued the trend of massive crowds following United in this season's competition with over 72,000 packing Everton's Goodison Park. In comparison to the first match, much more football was played and most of it from Manchester United, particularly in the first-half which they dominated.

They still though could not get past the excellent Wolverhampton goalkeeper Bert Williams though, and as the second-half unfolded Wolverhampton came much more into the game. With only 5 minutes left, a move towards the United goal seemed to have left the Wolverhampton centre-forward Jesse Pye in an offside position. The linesman disagreed though, and Pye went on to bring a save from Jack Crompton which fell into the path of Smyth who settled the tie and put Wolverhampton Wanderers into the FA Cup Final. The team followed captain Johnny's lead in accepting the controversial decision, another example of the hold and man management that Johnny possessed.

Figure 15 Footballer of the Year

The night before the final, Johnny and Matt Busby left the team, who were travelling north to play Newcastle United on the Final's day, to collect Johnny's Footballer of the Year award in London. They both then caught the overnight train north to Newcastle ready for the following day's First Division match. Showing all his composure, Johnny was the man of the match as United won 1-0 to keep themselves close to the top of the table.

They did stay close, achieving runners-up spot for the third consecutive season by beating league winners elect Portsmouth at Maine Road on the last day of the season. This would also be the last time Manchester United would need to use the neighbour's ground as their home stadium, because news had come through that Old Trafford had now been entirely rebuilt and approved to stage football league matches again from the start of the 1949-50 season.

> **Football Writers' Association: Footballer of the Year Award**
>
> The Football Writers' Association (FWA) was formed in 1947 following a discussion by journalists, Charles Buchan (News Chronicle), Frank Coles (Daily Telegraph), Roy Peskett (Daily Mail), and Archie Quick. The discussion took place aboard a boat in the middle of the English Channel that was returning from a football match in which England beat Belgium 5-2. Newspaper circulation at the time was huge, and the public relied on their favourite writers to keep them up-to-date with news on their favourite teams and players. Perhaps the most famous activity of the FWA is its annual Footballer of the Year Award. Charles Buchan, one of the founding fathers of the FWA, had originally suggested that there be an award presented *'to the professional player who by precept and example is considered by a ballot of members to be the footballer of the year.'* The award has always been considered the most prestigious award in English Football and the list of winners is an A-Z of legendary players. The first Footballer of the Year for the 1947-48 season was Stanley Matthews, and Johnny Carey was the second winner, the following season.
>
> At the time of writing, there have been 70 winners of the award. Johnny's win is notable for many reasons. Apart from the legendary Bert Trautmann in the 1955-56 season, Johnny was the only non-British winner of the award until Dutchman Frans Thiessen of Ipswich received the award 32 years later for the 1980-81 season. The only other Irishman to win the award is Roy Keane, some 51 years later. Lastly, along with joint winner Tony Book (with Dave Mackay) in the 1968-69 season and Steve Nichol 1988-89 he is one of only three out and out full-backs to win an award which generally goes to the more glamorous attacking players.

WORLD CUP 1950 QUALIFIERS

As already noted, Johnny had captained the IFA Ireland team in the British Championship which was also served as the qualifying competition for the 1950 World Cup Finals in Brazil. In his other position as part of the Dublin based Ireland team, Johnny was also able to take part in their qualification games too. They were drawn in Group Five along with two Scandinavian countries, Sweden and Finland. The matches, home and away had to be played by the end of 1949, and so after the end of the 1948-49 football season, Johnny would be involved in four internationals, one of which would be a World Cup qualifier against Sweden.

Before that, Belgium played a friendly in Dublin in late April 1949, a

Belgium side managed by Englishman Bill Gormlie who also managed their main club side R.S.C. Anderlecht. Seven years later he would lead them against Manchester United in the first European Cup tie played by an English team, with Joseph Mermans, also playing in the Ireland match of 1949, captaining Anderlecht in the European Cup match. Gormlie and Mermans had the last word in Dublin as they beat Ireland 2-0, they had a different outcome against United in 1956 losing the game in Manchester 10-0!

In late May 1949, perennial opposition Portugal visited Dublin to play Ireland in a friendly for the fourth time since the war. Portugal had won the first three, but a 1-0 Irish victory put them in great heart for their World Cup qualifier against Sweden. That was to be played in Stockholm in early June. Sweden were reigning Olympic Champions and had an excellent side at the time, they were too good for Ireland, winning 3-1 and staking an early claim to be Group Five winners. This seemed to dishearten Ireland and for once Johnny, who probably gave his worst ever performance in an Ireland shirt a couple of weeks later when Spain, another perennial friendly opponent for Ireland since the end of the war, visited Dublin.

The Spanish left-winger, Gainza, was in outstanding form and he gave Johnny a torrid time as Spain won comfortably 4-1. In his defence, Johnny had played nonstop since the previous August, playing 41 league matches, seven FA Cup ties, a Charity Shield and eight internationals split between the two Irelands. Oh, and he also had been presented with the Footballer of the Year trophy and taken Manchester United to a third successive runners-up spot in the league.

During the summer of 1949, Johnny took the first steps in preparing for a future after playing, as he completed a coaching course held at Birmingham University, conducted by his former teammate, and now England manager, Walter Winterbottom. This qualified him to supervise school football coaching, a task he would put to good use teaching his son Michael at his school St. Bede's College.

The World Cup campaign would end in chaos for the Dublin based Ireland. Firstly, after beating Finland 3-0 at home in September 1949, then gaining an excellent draw in Helsinki in the return, Finland suddenly pulled out of the World Cup, leaving just Sweden and Ireland in the group. This put everything on the return against Sweden in Dublin in November 1949. Sadly, after a great run of performances, the Swedish side, a very fine team it should be noted, won 3-1 to end the Brazil 1950 World Cup dreams for Ireland, and their one true world star Johnny Carey.

Suddenly, another door opened for Ireland though, when Scotland decided that they, like Finland, would not compete in Brazil in 1950. Ireland were offered their place, but in the end, the FAI felt the financial aspects were too severe and declined.

Chapter Six

BACK HOME AT OLD TRAFFORD

Even though the stands looked bleak and bare after the rubble had been cleared, for Manchester United supporters, there was no place like home, which was why the words, *Welcome Home'* were emblazoned over the cover of the opening two 'United Review' club programmes for the return to Old Trafford. Following the eight-year spell at Maine Road, the programme for the visit of Bolton Wanderers on Wednesday 24 August 1949 was the first for a Football League match at Old Trafford since the 26 August 1939 when Grimsby Town had provided the opposition in the only home league game of that season before the outbreak of the Second World War. United had started the season in real style by winning away at Derby County 1-0 on the previous Saturday, so a 3-0 home victory against Bolton Wanderers set Johnny and his men on their way in the 1949-50 season. Charlie Mitten scored the first goal back in front of an Old Trafford crowd of over 41,000. The local papers of the time reported huge congestion on the routes to the stadium as fans once again travelled to their spiritual home. West Bromwich Albion were the next visitors to Old Trafford, the following Saturday when the first points were dropped in a 1-1 draw. Following the traffic problems of the previous week, that issue of the 'United Review' provided a lot of information to remind people of the best transport routes to Old Trafford. The club didn't want fans returning to Maine Road. The various bus services were listed, as was information for the new Manchester United Railway Station with trains leaving Manchester Central from 1.45pm to 2.40pm, returning to the city from 4.35pm to 4.56pm at the cost of 6d (2.5p)

Figure 16 'Welcome Home!'

depending on the various kick-off times. Those people lucky enough to afford cars at the time were advised to use nearby Lancashire County Cricket Ground as the main car park.

50

Old Trafford

As Newton Heath Lancashire & Yorkshire Railway Company, Manchester United's first ground was located adjacent to the railway yard on North Road. The club were evicted in 1893 after their landlords (Manchester Deans & Canons) objected to spectators paying an entrance fee. The club then moved to Bank Street in Clayton which was gradually developed to a capacity of around 50,000. However, after United won the league in 1908 and the FA Cup in 1909, they grew more ambitious, and a new stadium named 'Old Trafford' was built. The initial aim was for this ground to have a capacity of 100,000 but in the end, the stadium's capacity was 77,000.

Old Trafford is now one of the most famous sporting venues in the world. It is named after the region of Manchester in which it is located – adjacent to Trafford Park, what was at the time one of the largest and most advanced manufacturing centres in the world. The importance of Trafford Park to the war effort made it a prime target for German bombing raids. The stadium was first hit in December 1940 in a strike that cost over a thousand lives around Manchester. The nearby Old Trafford Cricket Ground, home of Lancashire County Cricket Club suffered more severe damage that night, and the football ground was able to reopen after a couple of fixtures were played at Stockport County while repairs were conducted. The bomb damage that then occurred on Tuesday 11 March 1941 was much more severe though, and the ground would remain closed to first-team football until Wednesday 24 August 1949.

For the period when the ground was closed United relied on neighbours and rivals Manchester City's generosity in allowing them to share their ground at Maine Road. Manchester United were charged £5,000 per year, plus a nominal percentage of gate receipts. At the end of the war, United were able to claim £22,278 compensation from the War Damage Commission to rebuild Old Trafford.

The new ground was almost an open bowl, which was gradually developed with the addition of roofs. The roofs were supported by pillars that obstructed many fans' views, and they were eventually replaced with a cantilevered structure, with the first cantilevered stand being built by local firm Seddon's in time for the 1966 World Cup. The Stretford End was the last stand to receive a cantilevered roof, completed in time for the 1993–94 season at which point the ground became all-seater with a capacity of 44,000. Since this time further tiers and extensions have been added to bring the current capacity up to 75,957. Further development would mean extending the Sir Bobby Charlton Stand above the railway line which runs alongside the ground. Although this is frequently suggested, there are as yet no definite plans to commence what would be a major project.

The return home had the desired effect for Manchester United as they went undefeated in their first eight matches, although four of the games were draws. One of the victories was when Manchester City arrived at Old Trafford and were welcomed with a 2-1 United victory.

Following the eighth match undefeated, Johnny was off on his international duties, this time a highly significant one, as Ireland became the first country from outside Britain to beat England at home. The match was played at Goodison Park, home of Everton, on Wednesday 21 September 1949 before a crowd of 51,047, many expectant Irishmen amongst them! They were not to be disappointed, as Ireland secured a famous 2-0 victory.

As was anticipated, England put Ireland under severe pressure, Johnny marshalling his defence while trying to keep tabs on that brilliant footballer Tom Finney. Fellow defender, Con Martin and goalkeeper Tommy Godwin were in inspired form, indeed just past the half-hour mark, Martin had duties in the England penalty area as he converted a penalty to put Ireland in the lead 1-0. The second-half followed the same pattern, when with time running out, Peter Harris, an Evertonian playing for Ireland on his own club ground, put Ireland 2-0 up and secured a marvellous victory. Facing Johnny in the England side was his Manchester United full-back partner John Aston and former teammate, Johnny Morris now of Derby County.

Johnny remembered the memorable day, *'Whilst playing international football was always a great honour, both Ireland sides I represented had varying results, we always were the underdog to start with. I had been in Northern Ireland sides that had lost 7-2 and 6-2, so it was not necessarily with a lot of hope that we travelled to Goodison Park to play England for Ireland. It was one of those days when defensively we were all on our game, England missed chances, and we had a bit of the luck, the luck of the Irish. I heard that the people back home could not quite believe the result when they heard it, thinking the announcer had got it wrong!'*

Back with United after the euphoria of defeating England, Johnny concentrated on his one remaining dream, that of lifting the Football League Championship. After their excellent start, a couple of defeats stopped the flow, but by Christmas, United were in a challenging position near the top of the table, as the FA Cup also appeared on the horizon. Over that Christmas period, Manchester United went back to their 'old' home of Maine Road and showed they had lost none of their affection by recording a 2-1 victory over City.

As with the previous season in the FA Cup, a non-league side would be given the dream draw of a tie against United. This time it would be Weymouth who would be visiting Manchester, but now at Old Trafford. Football was a way of life for many people after the war. Even a team such as non-league Weymouth had as many as 4,000 members in their supporters club with over 500 travelling to Manchester for the club's biggest occasion. A 4-0 defeat still brought honour to the club, particularly as eight members of the Manchester United side that had beaten Blackpool at Wembley Stadium less than two years earlier played in this tie.

A fellow Irishman was in the Manchester United goal for the Weymouth cup tie, Ignatius (Sonny) Feehan, due to a severe hand injury sustained against Aston Villa by regular keeper Jack Crompton. Jack had played on for a few games before the full extent of his injury, a fractured wrist, was diagnosed, keeping him out for three months. A young replacement was signed from Darlington, Ray Wood, who had become the first of the side known as the 'Busby Babes' to make his debut. By the time the 4th round tie, away at Watford, arrived, Feehan was also injured so another young goalkeeper on the books, Joe Lancaster, was pressed into action. He more than did his bit as United ground out a 1-0 victory to give them a glamorous 5th round tie at home to champions Portsmouth.

Both sides had genuine thoughts of doing the 'double' that season, Portsmouth then lying just behind United in the league table and, of course, this being the 5th round of the cup the winner would have those thoughts hardened. Howling wind and pouring rain did not seem to be conducive to fine football from these two top sides, but that is what transpired. A two-goal lead at half-time for United seemed to have put them firmly in the driving seat until Portsmouth scored twice inside three minutes early in the second-half. Both sides then converted penalties to tie the match 3-3. The replay would be at Fratton Park, seemingly giving the advantage to Portsmouth. Johnny recalled the difficulties the defence was having due to goalkeeping changes. *Jack Crompton had always been a part of our side since the return in 1946, playing a great role in winning the FA Cup in 1948. He had made a great save in a match at Villa Park back in October from a Dickie Dorsett free-kick which he later wished he had missed as it caused so many problems with his wrist, which turned out to be fractured. 'Sonny' Feehan a fellow Irishman, stepped in, he then had an illness, meaning Joe Lancaster came in, which for the Portsmouth cup tie unsettled the defence, but it was not just Joe, a few of us played loosely and gave Portsmouth a chance back into the tie.'*

'Sonny' Feehan came back for the replay, but United were without Stan Pearson for the first time in three years due to a knock he received in the first match. Thankfully, the other forwards were in excellent form, and this time with the defence much sounder, United comfortably won the replay 3-1, and it was they who were serious contenders for the coveted league and cup 'double', a 'double' which hadn't been achieved that century though United had threatened a couple of times since the resumption of League football in 1946.

Only a point behind then leaders Liverpool, United went flat out to get League points before they would meet Chelsea away in the quarter-finals of the cup. Johnny would again be a very consistent performer that season, playing in 38 of the 42 League matches and being an ever-present in the FA Cup. Being a right-back his goals were now few and far between, but a valuable 15-yard winner at Charlton Athletic put the side top just a week before the cup tie at Chelsea. Although Johnny also got a goal for Ireland in a draw with Norway earlier in the season but was now concentrating more on helping his defence keep the opposition out.

Sadly, it would not be a return to Wembley Stadium though this season, as Manchester United surprisingly lost 2-0 to Chelsea before a 70,000 Stamford Bridge crowd in the 6th round of the cup. Whether a bit of complacency had crept in after excellent recent performances or not, there was no doubt United were poor in this match, not helped by a soft early goal being let in by the returning Jack Crompton. Indeed, it was only the two full-backs, Carey and Aston who played to their usual form as the side had a distinct off day.

A mid-week league match against Aston Villa at Old Trafford took on extra importance, firstly to bounce back from the cup defeat and secondly to keep right at the top of the league. Bounce back they did, with an emphatic 7-0 victory, containing the very unusual feat of a hat-trick of penalties being scored by one player, Charlie Mitten achieving this feat in his four-goal haul. When United then won 3-2 at Middlesbrough and held second-placed Liverpool to a 0-0 draw at Old Trafford, they were four points clear at the top of the table and hopes of that elusive league title grew. Certainly, Johnny felt so. *'I was now 31, and my chances of landing the league title was going to be fewer and fewer. We were in great form, albeit the disappointing defeat in the cup was hard to take, and felt we had real chance to win the title. What happened in those last games I honestly do not know.'*

Disappointingly, from a position of real strength, United then went eight matches without a single victory, only winning the last match of the season, at home to Fulham 3-0 before the lowest crowd of the season 11,968. This left them in fourth position in the final table, three points behind Portsmouth, who were champions for the second successive season. Local neighbours Manchester City were relegated, but the red side of Manchester seriously felt they had missed a big opportunity. The award of 'Sportsman of the Year' for Johnny was a very well-deserved accolade to a great man.

The players did have a six-week break to look forward to, as a few days after the season ended they set sail for America aboard the Queen Mary, sailing from Southampton, with Johnny turning his hand to writing as he extended his weekly column with the News Chronicle.

Johnny relished the opportunity to let readers back in Manchester read what life was like over in America and Canada on the United tour. While the team sailed over to New York, Johnny detailed the social activities the players had on board, with table tennis, darts and snooker competitions being keenly contested. When the Queen Mary landed, it was soon time to meet superstars such as Louis Armstrong at functions, while the sheer bustle of everyday life took Johnny's breath away. Indeed, Johnny referred to New York as *'Gadget*

Town' as everywhere you went *'there are machines to put a nickel in and try and get something out'*.

New York also was the scene for Johnny's typically self-deprecating Irish wit to come out. The team were being driven on a tour of the city when the bus stopped at a set of lights, right outside a large store called Cohen & O'Sullivan. Johnny pointed at the names saying *'I bet I know which of these two does all the hard work!'*

After acclimatising in America, it was across in Toronto, Canada, that the long football tour actually began. It would last six weeks during which time Manchester United played 12 matches across both countries, finishing in Chicago. Nobody would have guessed when they arrived, but one player, would not be going back with the team, he would be leaving for an entirely different financial world...

Most of the opposition would be called All-Star XL's made up of players from organised leagues or local cities. A couple of other sides from abroad, Besiktas from Turkey and Jornoping from Sweden would also play United, Jornoping twice, while the English FA Xl would also be an opponent just before they took part in the 1950 World Cup Finals in Brazil. United recorded some significant victories, 9-2 being one in New York, and of the 12 matches eight were won, two drawn and only two games ended in defeat. The two losses came in the last two games of a long tour, following a long English season, 4-2 against the FA XI and in the last tour game, 3-1 against Jonkoping, a Swedish side that United had beaten 4-0 earlier in the tour. One of the United scorers against the FA side was Charlie Mitten. This would be the last goal he would score for the club, as Charlie became one of the Columbian rebels who left English football for what was in comparison, thanks to the maximum wage, a life of luxury.

Earlier in the tour, Johnny had had real doubts this type of move would ever happen as he explained in his News Chronicle articles, headlined *'£3,500 a year does not tempt us'* the article said *'I recently received a telephone call informing me that an agent would be contacting me and other Manchester United footballers to persuade us to play in Columbia. None of the Manchester United players would consider the moves being discussed concerning the Columbian side Independiente Santa Fe trying to lure players stuck on the maximum wage in England with a life of luxury, or so it would seem. This proposition would mean they would never be able to play in Britain again, as Columbia were banned by F.I.F.A.'*

Charlie Mitten though was tempted, and he flew to Columbia to see what really was on offer. When he took the return flight, it was to Manchester and not New York to tell his wife and family that he had signed a deal worth seven times his salary in Manchester. He would never play for Manchester United again...

In some of his other articles, Johnny reported on the very glamorous style of life the United footballers had been introduced to while in America.

'We all had an experience we shall never forget. A visit to the MGM film studios in Hollywood meeting all the stars, it made a real change to see the spotlight on others rather than ourselves. For example, what seemed like another nice restaurant was full of film stars. Then, Clark Gable strode in and placed his Stetson on top of my cap! Ladies, he was a very handsome man who came over and welcomed us all to Hollywood.'

Tours to the USA always attracted the rich and famous of the day. Johnny treasured the autographed picture below, taken during a later tour, showing the team with another Hollywood star of the time, Jerry Lewis.

Figure 17 United on Tour in the USA (1952)

In another article, Johnny described playing in a floodlight match in New York which made a big impression on him. *'I firmly believe that floodlights would revolutionise the sporting scene in Britain if it was introduced here. My first sighting was at the Polo Grounds, the home of the famous baseball team, New York Giants. As the United team travelled in private cars through Harlem to the Polo Grounds, they were filled with an air of expectancy. When we got there, we were thrilled with the wonderful sights. As we looked out from our veranda outside the player's entrance, we could see so many families who had come to enjoy themselves. You just sensed this was the future of the game.'*

Back home, Johnny had a few weeks off before pre-season training started. Football news from America still filled the papers though, with news coming in of the shock 1-0 defeat of England by the USA in the Brazil World Cup. One of the star players for the USA team was wing-half Eddie McIlvenny, and in a surprise move, Matt Busby signed Eddie, a Scotsman who had qualified to play for the USA. In another transfer, the signing of experienced goalkeeper Reg Allen from Queens Park Rangers for a then record fee for a goalkeeper was felt by many to be the last piece of the jigsaw that would turn those four runners-up positions into the number one spot for Manchester United. It would be, but not in the 1950-51 season…

1950-51 SEASON

The three players mentioned in the last paragraph, Johnny Carey, Reg Allen and Eddie McIlvenny all appeared in the season opener against the side who had played the final fixture of the previous season, Fulham. In Allen and McIlvenny's case, it was for their Manchester United debuts while Johnny had missed the previous game with Fulham due to injury. There was a much-improved attendance from that match, with over 45,000 present at Old Trafford witnessing a Manchester United victory 1-0.

It soon became apparent though, that United would miss the play of Charlie Mitten on the left-wing, which gave Matt Busby early season headaches. Billy McGlen, a wing-half, was tried at number eleven for a few games before Matt Busby went into the transfer market and signed Harry McShane from Bolton Wanderers, with Johnny Ball going the other way plus cash. Ball was a very decent full-back, but with Johnny and John Aston still in such fine form, opportunities were rare.

Johnny was featured in the club programme the 'United Review' for the visit of Charlton Athletic. The brilliant cartoonist Butterworth reflected on a history of Manchester United that had just been written wondering why it had not gone back to the times of the Magna Carta, suggesting it was the signing on of Jonathan Carius, an ancestor of Johnny Carey!

The inconsistent form of the team also gave Matt concerns with victories being punctuated by defeats. In October a young Barnsley lad called Mark Jones had celebrated his debut in the home match against Sheffield Wednesday with a 3-1 win. Mark's appearance came because of the England debut for trusted centre-half Allenby Chilton, following on from the debuts of goalkeeper Ray Wood and young wing-half Jeff Whitefoot in the previous season as the first of the players who would become the team known as the 'Busby Babes' by the mid-1950's.

While the younger players were starting to appear, in November 1950 another of the famous 1948 FA Cup Final side departed. Jimmy Delaney, a marvellous Scottish winger who had instantly settled into the Manchester United way, decided to go back to play in Scotland for Aberdeen. So, in the space of six months, Manchester United had lost both of their wingers, Delaney and Mitten. Johnny though recalled the impact the younger players were starting to make at the club.

'Matt Busby and Jimmy Murphy had quickly identified during the 1946 season that, although they had a team of fine players, most of them had lost six years during the war and who would replace them? They changed their approach and searched the country for young talent. The appearance of young Mark Jones recently in such a vital position as centre-half showed if they were good enough they would be given a real chance.'

An injury to Johnny meant he missed the game at Huddersfield Town, this compounded by Jack Rowley going down with flu prompted Matt Busby to push John Aston to centre-forward as the team struggled to hit a level of form that would bring that elusive league championship back to Old Trafford. When the many fixtures of the Christmas period arrived, it was not just injuries and flu that were Matt Busby's problems. Three defeats, two of them at Old Trafford really rocked everyone connected with the club. The arrival of 1951 wholly changed the fortunes of the team and would lead to real success. The New Year heralded the start of the FA Cup, and United were once again given lower league opposition in the form of local Third Division North side Oldham Athletic. While not convincing, United progressed with a 4-1 victory, before playing their first league match of 1951 against the star side of the season so far, Tottenham Hotspur. This was the famous Arthur Rowe 'push and run' team which would eventually lift the title by four points from Manchester United, but it was United who won this match 2-1, continuing a run which would eventually stretch to 12 league matches unbeaten plus three FA Cup ties.

Leeds United, then in the Second Division were comfortably beaten 4-0 at Old Trafford in the 4th round of the FA Cup which brought a mouth-watering tie against Arsenal at Old Trafford. That brilliant writer H.D. 'Donny' Davies, who wrote under the name of 'Old International' wrote in his Manchester Guardian report that Manchester United's 1-0 victory over Arsenal in that tie *'was a mother and father of a belting'* which was decided by a fine Stan Pearson goal and surely made Manchester United favourites for the cup.'

United's long undefeated league run ended at Stoke City, one of only two defeats Manchester United suffered from the start of 1951 which put them firmly in contention for the title, sadly the other loss was in the 6th round of the FA Cup, away at the hands of Second Division Birmingham City. Like the famous FA Cup tie across Birmingham in 1948 when Aston Villa scored inside the first minute, Birmingham City did likewise in this 1951 tie. This time Manchester United could not reply. Matt Busby did though see a man who would become an integral part of his developing plans for the future - Johnny Berry the diminutive Birmingham City outside-right, who he would bring to Old Trafford in the following season. Johnny had memories of Johnny Berry from a previous season. *'Johnny Berry was a marvellous outside-right. Hugged his line, clever, beat full-backs with ease and got more than a few goals, indeed, I remembered a marvellous goal he had scored for Birmingham City towards the end of the previous season at Old Trafford, although his club would be relegated.'*

Despite those two defeats at Stoke and Birmingham, Manchester United had a tremendous run of form from January to the end of the season, falling short by four points to the eventual champions, Tottenham Hotspur. If only that form had started over the Christmas period when United suffered two home defeats and one away, that elusive title would have landed at Old Trafford. As it was, on a positive note, from the five seasons since football had recommenced after the war, the FA Cup and four runners-up spots had arrived at Old Trafford. On the negative side though, the nucleus of the team was getting older by the season and time was running out for many, including the club's finest ambassador, and one of the games finest footballers, Johnny Carey.

Johnny had, yet again, shown great consistency playing 39 of the 42 league fixtures and all four FA Cup ties. He did miss a most exciting friendly at the end of the season when United hosted Red Star Belgrade in a Festival of Britain match, with Red Star impressing everyone as the game ended in a 1-1 draw. This was the first time that foreign opposition had appeared at Old Trafford, what irony that when Red Star Belgrade returned in 1958, it would be part of the European Cup quarter-final tie in which the return leg would see the biggest disaster imaginable to hit Manchester United.

The reason Johnny missed the match with Red Star was that the day after he would captain Ireland, in their friendly with Argentina in Dublin, where a 40,000 crowd saw an excellent display by the Irish before they went down to a 1-0 defeat. A couple of weeks later, Johnny again captained Ireland but this time to an excellent 3-2 away victory in Oslo against Norway, the nation he had made his international debut against 14 years earlier. Now 32, Johnny spent the summer of 1951 seriously considering his footballing future. He felt that time was running out for his playing career and was beginning to consider if he wanted to stay in the game. The following season, however, would give him one of the biggest thrills in his career ...

Chapter Seven

CHAMPIONS AT LAST!

After finishing runners-up in four of the five seasons since the war, Manchester United finally won the title their team so richly deserved at the end of the 1951-52 season. This was United's first League title since 1911, and only the third in their history. Winning the title meant that their captain Johnny Carey completed the full range of personal honours that a footballer could achieve. Not only was he now captain of a League and FA Cup winning side, and captain of his country, but also Footballer of the Year and had captained a Rest of Europe XI. Amidst his success was an admiration of Johnny as a man. He was widely regarded as an elegant footballer and an unassuming man, his play seen as a model of artistry, skill and scrupulous fairness. All agreed that his calm, unflurried play and his influence as a captain were central to the success of Manchester United.

Back in 1951, the pre-season consisted of practice matches at Old Trafford between the first and second XI's following on from matches against two junior sides, both games known as the Reds v Blues. A very different preparation from staying in America or playing across the Far East for a month! The opening match of the season would be a game against West Bromwich Albion at the Hawthorns, surprisingly only attracting a crowd of just under 28,000. Indeed, those who came that day were well rewarded by goals, as the match finished in a 3-3 draw with United's centre-forward Jack Rowley starting off the season in explosive style with a hat-trick. As mentioned in the last chapter, the nucleus of the Manchester United side still involved up to six players from the victorious 1948 FA Cup Final side. Five of them appeared in this opening fixture at the Hawthorns, only Johnny Aston being unavailable. The team on the opening day of what would finally be a title-winning season was: Allen; Carey (capt); Redman; McGlen; Chilton; Cockburn; McShane; Downie; Rowley; Pearson and Bond. An interesting side note to this game and times: after the match Manchester United gave lifts home to six West Bromwich Albion players on the team coach, illustrating the rarity of car ownership by footballers at the time and lack of motorways such as the M6!

Jack Rowley is one of the all-time great Manchester United centre-forwards, and he did not stop with his opening day hat-trick. His final total for the season was 30 goals, but he started like a man on a mission with 14 goals in the first seven games including three hat-tricks! Early in the season, his supply line was further enhanced when Matt Busby went into the transfer market and brought right-winger Johnny Berry to the club from Birmingham City for £25,000, filling the space left by the departure the previous season of Jimmy Delaney to Aberdeen.

After the flying start, with a 'double' over Middlesbrough being followed by a 2-1 home win over Newcastle United in front of a 51,000 Old Trafford crowd, a first defeat arrived at Bolton Wanderers who won a fierce local derby 1-0 in a game that attracted 52,000 to Burnden Park. Johnny Berry scored his first Manchester United goal to win the match on United's return to Maine Road for the away match with City, before further defeats away at Tottenham Hotspur before a vast White Hart Lane attendance of 70,000 and the first home defeat to Preston North End by 2-1 occurred.

Johnny suffered a knock in mid-October meaning he would miss two crucial matches, a difficult away league game at Villa Park against Aston Villa and an Ireland friendly international in Dublin against Germany. Being the man he was, Johnny would have shared the joy of his teammates as both United, with a 5-2 away victory, after being 2-1 down at half-time, and Ireland with a famous 3-2 result secured much-needed victories.

The victory over Aston Villa put United top of the league, but the ups and downs of football meant that by the end of November, United would find themselves in seventh spot in the league after a terrible month. Of the four matches, two were drawn, and two lost, but in the fullness of time, it would be the catalyst for Manchester United to finally achieve the elusive dream they had fallen agonisingly short of for the past five seasons.

In the two draws, home to Huddersfield Town and away at Liverpool, Johnny was up against two of the finest outside-lefts he had ever faced. The Huddersfield Town match drew the lowest crowd to Old Trafford for the season 25,616 finishing in a disappointing 1-1 draw. The Huddersfield goal coming from a penalty scored by Vic Metcalfe. Johnny had a high opinion of Vic as he explains *'Vic was the type who takes the ball up to the full-back, flicks it some yards past you and then races, and he certainly could race, beyond you while you are still turning. The seconds you lost are all he needed and away he was.'* Vic Metcalfe was indeed a fine winger, but he only won two caps for England, showing the difficulty of breaking into the international side due to the consistency of Matthews and Finney on the wing positions, a problem also faced by United's new outside-right Johnny Berry.

UNITED'S "BABES" COOL, CONFIDENT
BY TOM JACKSON

IT was a case of on with the old—and the new—at Anfield this afternoon, where Manchester United, seeking their first victory this month, included four reserves in their line-up against an unchanged Liverpool team.

Figure 18 The birth of the "Babes"

Two defeats away to Chelsea and at Old Trafford against Portsmouth meant six defeats by the end of November. There would only be two more in the league over the next 27 matches as the title gradually became a reality. The away match at Liverpool prompted manager Matt Busby to make changes. Significantly those included introducing young players Roger Byrne at left-back and Jackie Blanchflower at right-half, also bringing back Jack Crompton for Reg Allen in goal, who was having a difficult time as the team's fortunes slumped. Interestingly, journalist Tom

Jackson of the Manchester Evening News was credited in his report that night for bringing the word 'Babes' into the context of Manchester United as his headline stated, *'United's "Babes" cool, confident.'*

Playing for Liverpool that day was another outside-left that Johnny really admired, Scotland international Billy Liddell *'Billy was a different sort of winger in that he was big and forceful. I always felt trying to play on top of him without upsetting the defensive balance of your team, but not get drawn away by him because you also needed to cover your goal.'*

The week after, Johnny was moved to right-half, a position that Matt Busby had found difficult to fill. In doing so, enabling United to get more from new winger Johnny Berry as Carey's prompting produced even more opportunities from the right-wing. Tommy McNulty came in at right-back and was a very steady performer for United, playing his part in the 3-1 win over Blackpool which kick-started a spectacular run of form for the team. The upturn in form included comprehensive wins against Arsenal away by 3-1 and a heavy 5-2 defeat of West Bromwich Albion at Old Trafford, results which put Manchester United top of the table as 1952 arrived. Would they be there in late April when the season ended?

FA Cup time arrived with a home match against Hull City, a team then near the bottom of the Second Division playing Manchester United, top of Division One. A shocking result and performance by United saw the East Yorkshire side leave with a famous 2-0 victory which scuppered any ideas of a return to Wembley, but which would at the end of the season, be seen as a possible blessing, in that it ensured that winning the League was the only priority.

The highest crowd of the season at Old Trafford 54,254, welcomed local rivals Manchester City to Old Trafford for a game that provided a quick opportunity to get the cup disappointment out of the way. The match also gave Johnny his first goal of the season. Now settled at right-half it helped United to a 1-1 draw which was at least improvement on the cup disaster of the previous week, and when Tottenham Hotspur were defeated at Old Trafford the week after, United consolidated their position as league leaders.

The whole country was in mourning on 6 February 1952 when it was announced that King George VI had died. A date which would become indelibly etched in the memories of all Manchester United followers six years later. Showing the high regard that Johnny was held, he was chosen to represent football at an event on the eve of the King's funeral in mid-February.

Back to captaining Manchester United, Johnny led the club to a succession of victories, although they still could not completely break free from their chasers in the league table, Arsenal, Tottenham Hotspur and Portsmouth. Indeed, when lowly Huddersfield Town scored a late winner at their Leeds Road ground to beat United 3-2, it ended a run of 16 league matches unbeaten and gave others hope of catching United. A crucial visit to Fratton Park to play Portsmouth was not helped by the inclusion of Stan Pearson and Jack Rowley in the England side facing Scotland at Hampden Park on the very same day. Pearson scored both of England's goals in a 2-1 victory before a crowd of 133,000. Sadly, for United, they badly missed the firepower up front at Portsmouth, losing for the second consecutive week, this time 1-0. This put Portsmouth equal with Manchester United at the top of the table along with Arsenal, all three sides on 48 points, and all with six matches to play. Would serial bridesmaids Manchester United once again miss out on the ultimate prize?

United's remaining fixtures were against Burnley home and away over Easter, Liverpool at home on Easter Saturday, a visit to the seaside to play Blackpool and finishing with two home games against London sides Chelsea and Arsenal, the Arsenal game a potential title decider. After rarely scoring goals in recent seasons, and having only one so far this season, Johnny chose his moment well and scored goals in two of those matches! Manchester United would draw the two away matches at Burnley and Blackpool and score emphatic victories at Old Trafford in the other four games, scoring 19 goals on the way. Johnny got his second goal of the season in the 6-1 home victory over Burnley on Easter Monday, but it was his third goal a week after, at home to Chelsea, that would prove to be the most memorable Old Trafford night of his career. Let Johnny tell us his own story;

'With all our near misses I was thinking this just has to be our time. Victories at home over Easter 4-0 against Liverpool and 6-1 against Burnley when I scored a rare goal, set the scene for the vital last two games at home to Chelsea and Arsenal. The game with Chelsea was arranged for a Monday night because they had been involved in an FA Cup Semi Final against Arsenal which went to a replay. We just had to win as Arsenal were playing the same night away at West Bromwich Albion.

Chelsea were a funny sort of side, you never knew just what to expect from them, and as they had lost their cup replay I was concerned they now would be really relaxed as they had nothing to play for, and we did! Still the time of no floodlights, so it was a tea time April kick off with luckily, the whole team getting into the game straight away. Stan Pearson had put us in front when something happened which I will never forget. I got the ball near my own goal and started moving towards the massive uncovered Stretford End, with all the Chelsea players fanning out marking my teammates, obviously knowing my poor scoring record! This left me just outside their penalty area when the ball seemed to just bounce right for my left foot, which sent it right into the top corner of the Chelsea net. At that moment the League Championship felt ours, the crowd were all on the feet cheering wildly.'

CAREY MADE THEM CHAMPIONS

[Newspaper clipping text, partially legible:] After 41 years the championship flag will fly over Old Trafford next season. Manchester United's 3-0 victory over Chelsea made them champions, miracles excepted. One man again stood out in this struggle of pulsating incidents. He was Johnny Carey, their polished half-back and captain who scored a wonderful goal in the 43rd minute with a powerful drive from 25 yards. From goalkeeper to wing forward, Manchester's individuals revealed superb craft on the heavy ground. Rowley and Pearson formed the rearend of United's attack and they created the first goal scored by Pearson in the 23rd minute. After dribbling round Ellis, Rowley passed to Pearson who shot from 25 yards. Then came Carey's goal and the interval. Three minutes after the interval Cockburn sent in another shot which was deflected by the Chelsea half-back, McKnight, into the roof of the net, as he tried to stop it. From that time on Chelsea were allowed a little more latitude, but United always had the answer to any of their moves. Carey, Chilton and Cockburn formed a magnificent middle line, and the work of the forwards, perfect in formation and execution, was only marred by Byrne failing with a penalty in the 89th minute.

Figure 19 Manchester Evening Chronicle

Johnny is too modest to relate that the crowd's cheers were reserved for him. A leading journalist of the time, Alf Clarke of the Manchester Evening Chronicle, commented that *'although having watched football for many years, I have never seen such a tribute which was accorded Johnny Carey when he scored United's second goal. They simply rose to the Manchester United captain. The crowd's affection for this world-class player visibly affected him.'*

Let us go back to Johnny's memories of that night *'Another rare goal, this time by Henry Cockburn gave us a 3-0 victory over Chelsea, and although Roger Byrne missed a last-minute penalty, with Arsenal not winning at West Bromwich Albion it meant, barring a mathematical impossibility, we were champions before the match on the following Saturday against them. Although an evening game, there was still no floodlights in those days so even after having the celebrations with the team after the game it was not too late when I got back home to Chorlton.'*

Johnny's route home, as he still did not have a car, was a brisk walk rubbing shoulders with exuberant United supporters on the way, all of them shouting *'well done'* to the inspiring United captain. He remembered walking into his house *'Margaret my wife informed me that she was putting the children to bed so would I mind doing the washing up! Thinking back, it was marvellous how you were brought back to earth in those days.'*

The United side that beat Chelsea that night further emphasised their credentials as champions by beating Arsenal 6-1 the following Saturday. The team was: Allen; McNulty; Aston; Carey (capt); Chilton; Cockburn; Berry; Downie; Rowley; Pearson and Byrne.

An interesting sideline to the memorable goal Johnny scored in the Chelsea match, came 14 years later when a young Manchester lad who had been in the Old Trafford crowd that night was on the same flight to Dublin as Johnny just after England had won the World Cup in 1966. That lad was World Cup winner Nobby Stiles, and he recalled noticing Johnny on the plane telling him how well he still remembered seeing that goal from his viewpoint perched high up on the scoreboard end of Old Trafford. He said Johnny described it in detail, exactly as a young Nobby Stiles had seen it!

Manchester United finished as worthy champions, winning 23 of the 42 league matches, drawing 11 and losing 8. They scored 95 goals and finished with 57 points, remember two points for a win. Johnny played 39 of the 42 games in the League that season, scoring those three goals and playing in the lone FA Cup tie. Perhaps that noted journalist Geoffrey Green, best summed up the effect Johnny had on Manchester United's success *'No man was more deserving than the captain Johnny Carey, a model captain and among the most complete and versatile footballers in history. At first glance with his thinning hair and thoughtful expression, he looked older than his true age.*

But there was no doubting his maturity. From the moment he led his side out, you got the impression that he was bringing out a pack of schoolboys who were to be put through their paces under his supervision. Not that he was overbearing, on the contrary. Yet there was something in his measured stately tread that engendered an instant feeling of respect and authority. Carey, the most generous of opponents, earned his plaudits to the end'.

Manchester United - Football League Champions

At the time of writing Manchester United have been League Champions a record-breaking total of 20 times. Their victory in 1952 was just the third in their history and their first for 41 years. The club's previous championships were in 1908 and 1911 and were punctuated with an FA Cup win in 1909 in a golden era for the club prior to World War One. Between the wars though, United were less successful. They became a yo-yo club, alternating between the 1st and 2nd divisions with their lowest ever league position being 20th in Division Two in 1934.

In 1952 with a League Title to add to their consistent league form since the war and their second FA Cup in 1948, it seemed that United were on the verge of the most successful period in their history. As discussed earlier, many of the team were coming towards the end of their careers and there was a slight pause before further triumphs, as Busby's long-term plans bore fruit with the legendary Busby Babes' first title in 1956. This was followed by a second title in 1957. The manner of their victories coupled with the youthfulness of the side led most to believe that United would dominate domestically for years to come. They were growing in experience in Europe too – it was surely only a matter of time before the European Cup was brought home to Manchester?

Munich shattered that beautiful dream. That Matt Busby and Jimmy Murphy kept that dream alive, steering United to further League titles in 1965 and 1967 provides a remarkable testament to their stoicism and courage. To top this with a triumph in the European Cup in 1968 is an incredible feat. Manchester United were on top of the footballing world, and no-one would have predicted at the time that United fans would have to wait 26 years for their next league title in 1993 under the guidance of Sir Alex Ferguson. What followed was a remarkable period of domination under a ruthlessly determined manager. In total Sir Alex won 13 League titles in the 20-year period between 1993 and 2013. These of course combined with two League and Cup doubles and the unique treble in 1999. All of this was in the future though in 1952. Slowly but surely though, Matt Busby that was building the foundations that future success would be built on.

The Manchester Guardian gave a rare honour to a footballer by giving him a glowing mention in their leader's column *'Not only has Manchester United been so consistent in the league, along with winning the FA Cup since the war, it has been captained in a way that is a lesson for many others. 'J. Carey, their captain, has been a model footballer, technically efficient, a hard worker, never giving in, without forgetting that he is a sportsman, an inspirer of the older players and a steadying influence of the younger players. A most modest man, he has now won every honour open to him.'*

The Manchester Guardian's match report from the Arsenal victory serves also to show the esteem in which Johnny was held by the fans. Writing as only he could, The Old International (Donny Davies) vividly described the scene. *'As Manchester United's Football Champions, chased by worshippers, raced from the field at the close of their 6-1 defeat of Arsenal at Old Trafford on Saturday the Beswick Prize Band hastily struck up a tune which it had been holding in reserve for five seasons past – "See the conquering hero comes" the paean alas ended in a stricken wail, as by strangulation: and red-faced bandsmen could be seen struggling for their lives to get out of the crowd, holding aloft tubas and trombones, cornets and euphoniums, lest these too should be crushed flat in the press. A wildly enthusiastic crowd surged round the entrance to the concrete tunnel which leads to the dressing room chanting "We want Carey - We want Carey" quite oblivious to the fact that the great man at that moment was probably in his birthday suit, and with the rest of his perspiring colleagues, immersed up to his neck in a hot soda bath.'*

Figure 20 A magnificent cake!

With the title wrapped up, for the second time in two years United, went on an extended tour of America, this time sailing across the Atlantic on the Queen Elizabeth. On the voyage over a dinner was held to celebrate the winning of the League title. Johnny wrote about the cake prepared to celebrate the title. *'It was a masterpiece of confectionary, iced in red and white and made to represent a football pitch, even having a sign behind one of the goals which read, 'United 6 Arsenal 1.'*

On the tour of America, United would play 12 fixtures of which they won the first ten matches then suffered two heavy defeats to the side that had finished runners-up to United, Tottenham Hotspur. Following meetings with such as Clark Gable in 1950, this time Bob Hope and Jerry Lewis were amongst the celebrities that the Manchester United party met. Johnny went on this tour and showed his versatility as he played at right-back, left-back, right-half and centre-half. While Johnny was in America, his Ireland side played two friendlies away from home against Austria and Spain, losing both 6-0. It seemed though nothing could stop the feeling of fulfilment that Johnny Carey and Manchester United now had, but what would come next?

Chapter Eight

THE END OF AN ERA

The 1952-53 season was disappointing for Manchester United, as they proved unable to respond to the challenge of being champions. At one stage in the season, United were 21st in the table after a 2-0 home defeat to Stoke City. They would finally finish in eighth position. Manchester United did win a trophy though, the Charity Shield at home against Newcastle United 4-2, although bizarrely it was watched by the lowest crowd of the season, 11,381. Johnny Carey yet again was a consistent performer throughout the season, playing a reduced total of 32 of the 42 League matches, all four FA Cup ties and the Charity Shield match.

Despite his consistency, Johnny announced his retirement at the end of the season, after being at Manchester United for 17 years. There was no doubt he was still good enough to have continued, but this season had seen the first ever FA Youth Cup competition, and Johnny could see at first hand the talent that was beginning to come through the system.

Johnny had a long while to consider his options. A long boat journey home from America gave him the opportunity to reflect on the advancement of all the young talent around him, his growing age and his ambitions to make a mark as a coach and manager. The young talent that Johnny observed was making great strides forward in the pre-season practice matches played at Old Trafford. In the junior game, the name of Duncan Edwards was heard for the first time as the 16-year-old Dudley lad, who had come with a glowing schoolboy international reputation, made his Old Trafford debut.

The first two league fixtures were a repeat of the last two fixtures of the previous championship winning season, with a home match against Chelsea and a game against Arsenal, although this time the game was played at Highbury as opposed to Old Trafford. A 2-0 victory over Chelsea seemed to promise further glory but defeats at Arsenal 2-1 and then surprisingly at local rivals Manchester City by the same scoreline burst the balloon. A couple of victories and a couple of draws settled things down before the first chance of a trophy came when Newcastle United as FA Cup holders visited Old Trafford to play Manchester United for the 1952 FA Charity Shield.

It seemed the Manchester public did not feel the urge to watch this attractive fixture as a season-low crowd of 11,381 turned up for the

Figure 21 United Review - Charity Shield

early Wednesday night kick off. A dominant second-half performance by United though, coming from a goal down to achieve a 4-2 victory gave Johnny another opportunity to lift a trophy, completing the treble of League Championship, FA Cup and now Charity Shield in which he had captained Manchester United to victory.

October 1953 was a memorable one for goalkeepers at Manchester United. Three different ones would start games, with Johnny taking over the green jersey in one of the matches! The month began with the always important fixture against Wolverhampton Wanderers. Jack Rowley scored two first-half goals for United against Bert Williams the Wolverhampton goalkeeper who had just been recalled to the England squad. Manchester United's goalkeeper, Reg Allen had high hopes that he might get an overdue call-up for England following his part in winning the League championship, and indeed his performance in the first-half was far better than Williams. Wolverhampton did draw level by half-time, but Allen's performance kept United in the match. Reg Allen had suffered severely during the Second World War, being captured in Germany and spending four years in an unforgiving prisoner of war camp. We can only imagine what he had to go through, and at times this caused him lots of distress as he constantly fought to get his life back on an even keel. When somebody announced at half-time that Reg Allen had been overlooked and Williams had been called in as back up for England's forthcoming international it had a profound effect on him. His frustration seemed to bring back all his old symptoms, and he was far too upset to take his place in the second-half. No substitutions of course in those days, so Matt Busby calmly told Johnny to take over the goalkeeper's jersey whilst everybody's thoughts were with a clearly unwell Reg Allen.

Wolverhampton Wanderers were an excellent side and they quickly smelt blood at United's problems. Going in front in the first minute of the second-half, by 55 minutes the score was 5-2 in their favour and game over. A late goal compounded Manchester United's afternoon, but the 6-2 scoreline does not tell the sadness of this match, which turned out to be the final game in Manchester United's goal for Reg Allen.

The following week, young Ray Wood was recalled to the goal for the visit of Stoke City with Johnny reverting to his right-half position. A poor performance by all the team saw Stoke earn a 2-0 victory leaving Manchester United in 21st position in the league, with only local rivals Manchester City below them in the table.

A visit to Preston North End saw the third goalkeeper in three weeks for United as Jack Crompton returned. The 1952-53 First Division title race eventually produced the closest possible outcome imaginable, as Arsenal would finish above Preston North End on goal average by just a tenth of a goal! Both sides won 21 times in their 42-match season, drew 12 and lost 9 to finish on 54 points (two points for a win in those days). Arsenal scored 97 goals and conceded 64, while Preston North End scored 85 and conceded 60. With the title in those days based on goal average as opposed to goal difference, Arsenal had the slenderest of advantages. Manchester United played a significant part in determining the destiny of the title, as over their two fixtures with Preston North End, they would score TEN goals which would make all the difference to the final title calculations.

The first match in mid-October would see Jack Crompton a virtual spectator in the first-half as he looked on with the same astonishment as the 33,502 strong crowd who witnessed Manchester United go into half-time with a 5-0 advantage. In the second-half, Preston switched their talisman Tom Finney over to Johnny's side but found the way forward closed to him as United eased through the second-half to complete a very surprising scoreline. As we will see later in this chapter, another five-goal United victory, this time 5-2 in early March would prove significant for both clubs, providing the debut of a future Busby Babe for Manchester United and another damaging goals-against score for Preston North End as they fought for the title. A future Manchester United manager, Tommy Docherty, played in both these matches for Preston North End.

In mid-November 1952, Johnny played for Ireland against France in Dublin, a match that finished 1-1, but would cost him a couple of Manchester United appearances due to an injury he received. He had already missed United's visit to Cardiff City to play for Ireland in the France match, his injury meant he would miss the subsequent games against Newcastle United and West Bromwich Albion.

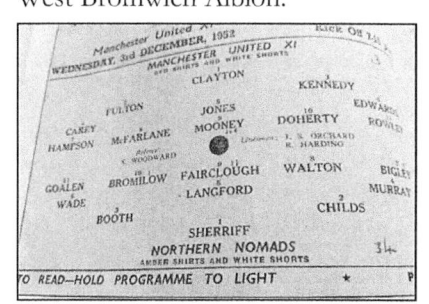

Figure 22 What a line-up!

To test if he would be fit to play against Middlesbrough at Old Trafford in early December, Johnny, together with Jack Rowley, was selected in a team of young players to play a floodlight friendly at the Cliff against the famous amateur side, Northern Nomads. What was extra special though for Manchester United would be that alongside those two greats of the club, a 16-year-old Duncan Edwards was playing alongside Johnny and another promising young player, Mark Jones, in the half-back line.

The Manchester Guardian reported this match in full, noting that, *'Carey and Rowley did sufficient to note they should return for Manchester United on Saturday against Middlesbrough at Old Trafford. Their occasional masterly touch did not disappoint but what was noticeable was the powerful performance of young Duncan Edwards at left-half. Edwards is remarkably strong for his age, fast and tackled well also possessing a powerful shot which Rowley would have been proud of.'*

Johnny was fit to play against Middlesbrough as Matt Busby took the opportunity to give two more of his promising young players their debuts, John Doherty an inside-right and David Pegg, a very accomplished left-winger. It all helped to give United a 3-2 victory as they slowly but surely climbed the table from the depths of the bottom two in early October. The week after, yet another young player, Bill Foulkes would play his first Manchester United game, away at Liverpool which produced another victory, this time 2-1.

A visit to London to play Chelsea would see Johnny take over in goal for the second time this season, this time with a much better ending than against Wolverhampton Wanderers. Johnny recalled the game, *'We had started to settle down a bit in the league after a poor start but were still too far off the top really to make a proper challenge. Matt Busby also was bringing more and more of his promising youth players in to keep all of us on our toes. When we played at Chelsea on the Saturday before Christmas, we went 3-0 up with young John Doherty getting his first goal for the team. Everything seemed rosy until Jack Crompton got a whack on his head and had to go off with concussion. As captain, there was nothing for it than to put on the green goalkeeper's jersey and hope for the best! We lost a couple of goals before securing a 4-2 win late on. It was a very happy journey home with me starting the singing!'*

John Doherty in recalling his first goal remembered a moment the week after when Johnny gave him excellent advice. *'I was in a hurry to get away one day from Old Trafford when a fan asked me to sign a programme. I said, "Can't stop, got a bus to catch". The day after, Johnny pulled me to one side at our training ground and said he had seen me refuse to sign the autograph. I mentioned I had a bus to catch, but he replied, "Son, there'll come a time when nobody asks for your autograph, so sign them all while you can." That was very sound advice, Johnny knew it was the fans who pay the wages, and you should offer them courtesy.'*

A rare goal for Johnny on Boxing Day at Old Trafford against Blackpool gave United a 2-1 victory and continued the good run for the team who had now climbed to eighth position as New Year arrived. The FA Cup seemed to offer Johnny his last chance of any silverware this season and the draw for the 3rd round away at Third Division South Millwall seemed a promising start. A Stan Pearson goal won a closer tie than many thought, resulting in one of those glamour ties that characterise the FA Cup, a real giant killing match-up as non-league Walthamstow Avenue were drawn to play at Old Trafford against the current League champions, Manchester United.

The all amateur Walthamstow side did have one famous sportsman in their team a certain T.E.Bailey, playing on the right-wing. Later in 1953, as cricketer Trevor Bailey, he would help England recover The Ashes when Australia toured. On the 31 January 1953, he helped Walthamstow achieve a remarkable 1-1 draw at Old Trafford!

The replay caused tremendous excitement in the country and was switched to Highbury, home of Arsenal, attracting a crowd of well over

40,000. Walthamstow fought just as hard, but this time Manchester United were in a much stronger mood and ran out 5-2 victors to give them an away tie in the 5th round at Everton, who were then in the Second Division.

Everton had a long, proud history, founder members of the Football League and this spell in the Second Division caused them great pain. Their fans were very loyal, and for the visit of Manchester United, a massive crowd of just under 78,000 packed out Goodison Park in mid-February 1953. United went into the tie in decent form, and captain Johnny Carey was desperate to get his side through on the ground where he had captained his native Ireland to a famous 2-0 victory over England four years earlier. A tough match could have gone either way, as Jack Rowley for United and Dave Hickson for Everton traded goals. It was to be heartbreak for Johnny though, as his Ireland teammate Tommy Eglington scored the decisive second goal for Everton to put them through to the 6th round of the cup and end Johnny's Wembley dream.

A visit to Roker Park, former home of Sunderland, used to be one of the stiffest tests for a side, a raucous crowd, probably a windy day coming off the nearby sea, so you can imagine Johnny's thoughts on 18 February 1953 as Manchester United travelled there from their overnight stay in Durham. Oh, and he had then been told that he would be playing the WHOLE match as the Manchester United goalkeeper!

This all came about when Jack Crompton reported feeling unwell with flu on the morning of the match. United had taken a squad of 12 players, no substitutes allowed in those days, but by 10am when the doctor advised Matt Busby that Crompton would not recover in time and that there was no way anybody could be sent from Manchester in time for the 2pm kick-off. The only option was to turn to his ever-reliable captain for yet another position for him to fill.

Let us hear what Johnny thought about this, *Jack Crompton was really unwell with a bad dose of flu, so Matt Busby looked at me and said, "you will have to play in goal!" Ok, I was 5'10 and 10st 11lb, but Roker Park was generally a hard game, and in Trevor Ford, they had a very dangerous centre-forward. We had a couple of very young players in Eddie Lewis and David Pegg, so it was always going to be difficult. Incredibly, we all turned on a very fine display with both those young lads getting a goal each, before, with less than ten minutes to go, I conceded an own goal from Allenby Chilton who simply sent a blockbusting header past me, and into his own goal!*

It looked as though we may have got an incredible victory when I made a bad mistake missing a cross over a crowd of players. I was feeling very happy with myself helping get a 2-2 draw until our trainer, Tom Curry, came into the dressing room and said, 'if it had been a bale of hay going through the goal you would not have even got a couple of handfuls!'

Perhaps sensing that Johnny was thinking more and more about his future, Matt Busby suggested he go and have a look at a player Manchester United might be interested in, a centre-forward called Tommy Taylor who was playing for Barnsley. Again, let Johnny tell the story, *'Matt asked me to go over to Filbert Street Leicester to see this centre-forward of Barnsley who was scoring a lot of goals. I reported back that he was very impressive and would be a good addition for Manchester United. Matt looked across to me and said, "that's good, you have just confirmed the other eight recommendations I had"!'*

Johnny was very pleased when United backed his view and signed Tommy Taylor. The fee was the unusual figure of £29,999 so that he was not burdened with the label of the first £30,000 player. He would turn out to be one of the greatest centre-forwards in Manchester United's history. Johnny was asked by Matt Busby to go along with him and meet Tommy Taylor as he arrived in Manchester by train, Johnny quickly noticing Tommy carrying his boots in a brown parcel and taking them off him, away from the prying eyes off the waiting photographers.

The much-awaited debut for Tommy Taylor came on 7 March 1953 at Old Trafford against Preston North End, a match which, as mentioned previously, would be crucial at the end of the season for Preston. Johnny had missed the previous game due to injury but was fit to captain the Manchester United side which saw the debut of the much-vaunted centre-forward, a player Preston North End themselves had looked at very earnestly.

The highest home crowd for the season, 52,590, filled Old Trafford with real optimism at the arrival of this exciting addition to the team. The signing of Tommy Taylor added to the experience the younger players were gaining, suggested a very promising future for Manchester United. It was not, however, the new number nine who threatened early on, but Johnny whose shot hit the bar, followed by another effort that was cleared off the line. Then the dream start for Tommy Taylor occurred as he put United 1-0 up. Tommy would score again in the second-half with David Pegg getting two as United won 5-2, a scoreline which was vital to Preston a few weeks later as they lost the league by a tenth of a goal.

Wednesday 25 March 1953 turned out to be Johnny's last appearance for the Republic of Ireland. The match in Dublin against Austria drew a crowd of 40,000 to see the Irish win 4-0, avenging their hammering in Vienna the previous May. None of the crowd, and quite possibly Johnny himself, knew it would be his 29th and final appearance for Ireland as he had not yet made an announcement about his future, but that would come soon…

Frank O'Farrell played for Ireland in this match, Frank, of course, would be a Manchester United manager 20 years on. Another player in the team this day was Tommy Eglington whose goal knocked Manchester United out of the FA Cup a month earlier, and he was on the scoresheet this day in Ireland's emphatic victory. As it turned out, a fitting end to all Johnny's efforts in making his country a worthy international team.

In the first two weeks of April 1953, two future stars for Manchester United would make their debuts. Good Friday had seen United play at

Charlton Athletic coming away with a deserved draw. Johnny, sadly, suffered a knock and with a quick turn round for the Easter Saturday fixture could not recover in time for the match with Cardiff City. Matt Busby decided that his 16-year-old prodigy, Duncan Edwards was already more than capable of making his league debut. Duncan did well, but sadly, United as a team had a miserable afternoon and surprisingly lost 4-1 at Old Trafford. There would be many better days for young Duncan, although football and Manchester United were to lose one of the game's greatest players far too young…

On 11 April 1953 another of the Busby Babes made his debut, Dennis Viollet playing at outside-right away at Newcastle United. Dennis shared in a fine 2-1 victory and later in his life recalled his memory of the match. *'Whilst I knew Jeff Whitefoot from schoolboy times, to be alongside heroes of the 1948 FA Cup Final was for me, a Manchester lad, a marvellous occasion. Allenby Chilton, Jack Rowley, Johnny Aston, my schoolboy hero Stan Pearson and, of course, the skipper Johnny Carey.'*

'They were all great with me before the kick-off, Johnny Carey was ever so polite and kind, shaking my hand and wishing me well. I immediately got on with Tommy Taylor, and he scored two cracking goals.' Dennis Viollet, who would turn out to be one of the great forwards for Manchester United, became the ninth player to appear in United's first team of what would be the accepted line up for Matt Busby's incomparable young side three years on.

As the season came to a close Manchester United finished in a disappointing eighth position one year after being league champions. They had departed the FA Cup in the fifth round, but at least won a trophy in the form of the Charity Shield. Discussion began to appear in the press about the future of some of the fine stalwarts that had led the club to so much success since the war. Johnny was at the top of the names discussed. He was the man who embodied everything good about Manchester United and was now 34. Even so, his form and fitness had been good throughout the season.

Johnny himself though could see at first hand the startling progress of the Manchester United FA Youth Cup side who had taken the competition by storm in its first season. He saw that there lay a glorious future for the club and had to consider his options. These included carrying on playing, joining the club's coaching staff or moving into management himself. The coaching staff option seemed a closed door, both Matt Busby and Jimmy Murphy were still young men really, so prospects for advancement at Old Trafford looked bleak, even though Manchester United still wanted to hold on to a man admired by everyone in football for his considerable influence both on and off the pitch. Tom Jackson, the Manchester Evening News reporter, was one of the first to raise the unthinkable, asking whether Johnny would still be a Manchester United player the following season. Johnny told Tom Jackson of his feelings. *'My future as a player hangs in the balance. I am not getting any younger, and I don't intend to become a "has been" in the game which has been my life.'*

Johnny had not made any official announcement as United moved into their last two matches of the season at home to Liverpool and a final league game at Middlesbrough. They would also be playing in the Coronation Cup in Scotland where four English and four Scottish teams would meet as the whole country got ready to celebrate the Coronation of Queen Elizabeth II in early June 1953.

> ### The FA Youth Cup
>
> The FA Youth Cup was held for the first time in the 1952-53 season. A youth cup competition was the idea of Sir Joe Richards. Joe was a former President of the Football League, and so he first proposed the idea to Football League clubs. The clubs were not receptive though, and so Joe then turned to the FA. The FA were much more enthusiastic and ran the first competition that year. The early years of the Trophy were dominated by Manchester United, who with a total of 10 victories remain the Trophy's most successful club.
>
> The timing of the competition was perfect for Manchester United. Even before the war, the club had begun to focus their efforts on the development of young players. Now, under the management of Matt Busby, the plan was going to unfold spectacularly in the form of the Busby Babes. The first signs of things to come were seen clearly in the FA Youth Cup, which United won for the first five years of the competition. The competition provided the canvas upon which the likes of Duncan Edwards, Bobby Charlton, Liam Whelan, David Pegg and Eddie Colman would first practice their art, as United's emphasis on youth provided what seemed an endless pipeline of talent into the first team. Finals were played over two legs, with the aggregate margin of victory for the first final against Wolverhampton Wanderers being 9 goals to 3. Wolves were a football powerhouse at the time, and were again the runners-up the following year, by the closer margin of 5-4. The next three finalists were West Bromwich Albion, Chesterfield and West Ham beaten by totals of 7-1, 4-3 and 8-2 respectively. United would have again been favourites for the following year's competition, but the Munich Disaster meant that youth players were needed for first team football, and so Wolves became the second team to win the trophy defeating Chelsea on aggregate by 7 goals to 6. It would be 1964 before United won the competition again, this time with a team that included George Best. Their next victory in 1992 was followed by runners-up spot the following year with a remarkable squad that famously dispelled the notion that you will 'never win anything with kids', as Ryan Giggs, Paul Scholes, David Beckham, Nicky Butt and the Neville brothers formed the nucleus of United's all-conquering treble side in 1999.
>
> In more recent times the path to first team glory for FA Youth Cup finalists has been less assured. Chelsea have repeated the feat of winning five successive competitions between 2014-18, though with less success in developing new players. Nevertheless, the recent World Cup Finals (2018) featured four FA Youth Cup Winners: Paul Pogba and Jessie Lingard from Manchester United plus Ruben Loftus-Cheek and Andreas Christensen from Chelsea.

The Liverpool match was played on a Monday evening in late April, and sadly, a small crowd of just 22,645 turned up, still, of course, unaware of Johnny's future. Johnny was now firmly back in the right-half position, and he helped steer his side to a fine 3-1 victory thanks to goals from Jack Rowley, Johnny Berry and Stan Pearson. Despite this being his last home league match, Old Trafford would get a couple more chances to see the majesty that was Johnny Carey when he appeared in Tom Curry's testimonial in September 1953 and in the Johnny Aston testimonial in 1956.

Figure 23 Boro escape the drop.

Saturday 25 April 1953 saw the last league appearance for Johnny in a Manchester United shirt when the team visited Ayresome Park, Middlesbrough to face a side who were still flirting dangerously with relegation as the last day of the season arrived. You would have wondered who the side near the bottom were, as Middlesbrough thumped a strong Manchester United side 5-0 to give Johnny an unfitting end to his glittering Manchester United career. Middlesbrough did have Wilf Mannion in their team, and that fine inside-forward scored two of their goals, along with creating their fifth with an audacious backheel to set up Arthur Fitzsimons, a teammate of Johnny in the Ireland side score with a header to make it 5-0. The Manchester United side for Johnny's last league game for Manchester United was: Crompton; McNulty; Aston; Carey (capt); Chilton; Whitefoot; Berry; Rowley; Taylor; Viollet and Byrne.

It was appropriate that as the career of one of football's truly great players came to an end, Old Trafford would see the arrival of another player who would become a legend, before his time at Manchester United was so cruelly cut short before his prime. Like Johnny, that person would be a man of Dublin, making his arrival even more poignant. He was William Augustine Whelan; whose first name was the chief topic of conversation as Johnny was asked to meet him as he alighted from the train in Manchester in early May 1953.

Whelan had been quickly recruited to take the place of inside-forward John Doherty for the first-leg of the first FA Youth Cup Final at Old Trafford between United and Wolverhampton Wanderers.

Johnny was quick to give him advice about Mancunians. *'I said to him "whatever you do hold onto your name!" That was because, in Ireland, William would be shortened to the last four letters making it Liam, whilst in England, William was known as Billy. I told him they had me known as Johnny or Jackie very quickly whilst, of course, my name actually was John.'*

When you look through Manchester United's history you will see Johnny was correct, Whelan is almost always known as Billy, only occasionally as Liam and never as William!

As an aside, Manchester United would win that first FA Youth Cup Final and, indeed, go on to win it for the first five years of its existence as they seemingly produced quality youngsters at the flick of a switch. Included in the side alongside newcomer Billy Whelan were such as Eddie Colman, David Pegg, Albert Scanlon and the incomparable Duncan Edwards, whilst Ronnie Cope and Eddie Lewis also had excellent first-class careers. Eddie Lewis would play a role in Johnny's future ten years on…

With this sort of talent coming through, Johnny was left with a tantalising decision. Did he stick around for another couple of years and see the youngsters fully develop, or move on himself to another career in football?

Before any official announcement was made, Johnny still had two more games to play in a Manchester United shirt as he captained the team in the Coronation Cup competition staged in Glasgow in mid-May 1953. United were drawn to play Glasgow Rangers at Hampden Park and Johnny, typically, put in a man of the match display as he led his side from a goal down to win 2-1, before switching to right-half for the semi-final against the other Glasgow side, Celtic.

Celtic had legends such as Jock Stein and Bobby Collins playing that day, but it was left-winger Charlie Tully who was the star for Celtic creating both their goals from Peacock and Mochan. Jack Rowley did get a late goal for United, fittingly from a Johnny Carey cross, but the majority of the 73,000 went home happy. The Glasgow Herald reported that Peacock had caused Johnny problems on the day whilst also commenting disapprovingly on several Republic of Ireland flags in the crowd. Glasgow Celtic went onto win the competition beating fellow Scottish side Hibernian 2-0 in the final.

The Coronation of Queen Elizabeth II marked a turning point in Britain. A growing number of people had access to their own television sets, which with the Butler Education Act of 1944 fully implemented, started to open the eyes of many bright young working-class children - as it gave them free education, and an opportunity to question the old order. While television had arrived, it would be another 50 years before such as Twitter, Facebook and the 24-hour saturation of talking about sport on both mediums of radio and television was part of everybody's life. In football, the players were always perceived as team players with the obvious better ones catching the eye, the advent of television from the 1960's onwards created the personality syndrome which nowadays has exploded far too much.

Johnny Carey played 304 League matches for Manchester United scoring

17 goals, along with 38 FA Cup matches with one further goal, along with two Charity Shield games. He led Manchester United to the Football League Championship and the FA Cup. One of a notable few Irishmen to represent both the Northern and Southern based international sides, Johnny captained both with distinction, playing 29 appearances for Ireland scoring three goals, and seven full appearances for IFA Ireland, as well as two Victory Internationals. He won the Footballer of the Year award in 1949, only the second man to have done so, while he captained the Rest of Europe against Great Britain in 1947.

The end of this incredible career was officially announced on 23 May 1953 to Tom Jackson in the Manchester Evening News. *There comes a time when you have to make decisions, and whilst I knew I could probably have played another year, possibly two, I felt the only way was going down. Matt Busby, the directors, staff, players and of course the supporters have been great to me, but I just feel now is the time. I have had a very full career, although those six lost years, which of course affected so many, had taken so much away. I had set standards and did not see me playing in the Second or Third Divisions. You only have to see the young players coming through already at Old Trafford into the first team with huge talent. This year from the back, I have seen at first hand Ray Wood, Bill Foulkes, Roger Byrne, Jeff Whitefoot, Mark Jones, Duncan Edwards, Tommy Taylor, Dennis Viollet and David Pegg. Manchester United's future is very bright indeed.'*

Tom Jackson, the Manchester Evening News reporter, added his appreciation. *'So, Johnny Carey, the man who has always lived up to the title of "Soccer's first gentleman", has played his last game for United. Soccer will be indeed all the poorer without this modest, almost self-effacing Irishman who has proved such a wonderful inspiration to the team he has captained throughout all their great post-war years.'*

The Old International writing in the Manchester Guardian penned this wonderfully insightful tribute:

John Carey, it seems, at the tender age of 34, confesses himself so conscious of the drag of advancing years on his once supple limbs that he has decided to quit the stage which he has graced for so long and retire at once from active football. This news will give rise to as many querulous farewells as there be stars in heaven, for Carey was and is admired as much for his charming personal qualities as for his skill. The temptation to continue must have been a strong one. For Carey is still a young man as the world goes and, as the world thinks, is still in his prime. But two considerations may have weighed with his generous nature—the reluctance to continue in the public eye for a day longer than he could guarantee a flawless performance and the fear that after 17 seasons of success and pleasure for himself, to stay longer might deny similar privileges to others. It is no new thing for great players to seem afraid to outstay their welcomes. Ernest Tyldesley, of Lancashire, and Frank Swift, of Manchester City, both retired before we could well spare them: and in retiring like them with his reputation still at or near its meridian, Carey will at least escape those gibes and taunts with which impatient crowds chivvy their flagging "old has-beens" however eminent. And, after all, when a player has won most of the honours which Association football can bestow— 36 international caps, a cup winner's medal, a championship medal, a silver trophy as Footballer of the Year, and, best prize of all, universal esteem — it is natural that he should want to carry with him into retirement the memory of the game's brightest honours and not its indignities. It was in the direction of his extraordinary versatility where Carey may be said to have crossed the borderline between talent and genius and to have rendered his greatest services to Manchester United and to Eire. Only once previously has Carey's versatility ever been approached and that was by the great Crabtree, formerly of Aston Villa: but whereas Crabtree's resources enabled him to fill both back positions and all three half-back positions for England at various times Carey was able to add to these variations one or two forward positions as well. Even as a forward, where his leisurely running style was somewhat deceptive, Carey was good enough to win international honours, but no sooner had he revealed his powers as a right-back than he took his rightful place as a leader among internationals, as the leader of the Rest of Europe against Britain, in fact. The uncovering of Carey's skill, first as a right-back and later as a right-wing half-back, were the two luckiest strokes of Mr Busby's management of the United during the past seven years. Much could be written about Carey's characteristics as a defender: how astute his sense of positioning how cleverly he diverted advancing opponents outward and ever outwards towards the wing: how he preferred to run alongside an opponent, waiting for a slip, rather than risk all in a desperate lunging tackle: how judiciously he took up position near a crowded goal. To these qualities, he added a deftness of touch and an adroitness in the use of the ball which place him securely among the finest artistic defenders of all time. Yet even here the tally is not complete, for he possessed that cool, calm, equable temperament, especially in moments of adversity, which marks the perfect leader. It goes without saying that in the fierce struggles for the Cup in 1948, and in the long trail for the championship in 1952, situations arose which tested Carey's captaincy to the full. It is to the credit of the man that he rallied his colleagues so frequently into retrieving bad starts, and only through an unswerving reliance on common sense methods and pure football. Like Marshal Foch, Carey had one outstanding merit—that of never despairing.'

On the announcement of Johnny's retirement, the Manchester United directors took the unprecedented gesture of inviting him into their boardroom to express their gratitude and appreciation of his service back to 1937, along with his massive contributions to the game of football. It is worth repeating the minute which recorded the tribute. 'The Directors expressed their deepest regret at his decision to end his playing career and unanimously agreed to put on record their great appreciation of his long and loyal service. But his outstanding personality as a true sportsman, the honours he had won as an international and in club matches, he has covered his whole career with glory and set a shining example to all who follow him.'

The question on the lips of all football fans was just where Johnny Carey would be in the 1953-4 season…

Chapter Nine

A NEW LIFE AT BLACKBURN ROVERS

The distance from the Old Trafford home of Manchester United, to Ewood Park, home of Blackburn Rovers is just 35 miles. In the footballing world of 1953 the two clubs were light years apart. Blackburn Rovers were founder members of the Football League and had, particularly in the early days of the FA Cup, become a famous name in the game. By 1953 though, they had become a regular Second Division side, and it would be with them that Johnny was offered the opportunity to start his managerial career shortly after announcing his retirement.

Johnny took over from former England international Jackie Bestall, becoming Blackburn's fifth manager since the war. He soon felt he needed to be as much a coach as a manager behind his office desk. When he arrived at Ewood Park, Johnny inherited an experienced side. Like Manchester United after the war though, they were an ageing side. Indeed, if he had taken his place in the team Johnny would have been the outstanding player even though he was now 34. He decided to employ a fast, open style of football while also looking to develop, in time, a youth policy, both features of course of the philosophy of his mentor Matt Busby when he had arrived at Old Trafford in 1945.

Figure 24 Johnny at his desk.

Amongst the players Johnny inherited were: Bill Eckersley the current England left-back; Eddie Quigley, once the most expensive player in Britain, who had moved from Sheffield Wednesday to Preston North End for £26,000 only four years earlier; Eddie Crossan a fellow Irishman; Tommy Briggs a free-scoring centre-forward and a couple of young players Ronnie Clayton and Bryan Douglas who would both develop to be amongst Blackburn Rovers greatest ever footballers.

The merging of Johnny's football philosophy with the existing Blackburn Rovers players seemed to have an immediate effect, as the team won 4-1 at Rotherham United in the 1953-54 season opener. Another couple of victories turned out to be the calm before the storm however, as Blackburn Rovers would suffer an embarrassing 8-0 defeat away at Lincoln City, equalling the Rovers worst ever defeat by the same score to Arsenal in 1933.

That defeat to Lincoln rushed Johnny into a signing, as he recruited left-winger Bobby Langton from Bolton Wanderers. Langton had played for

Blackburn previously. He had represented Bolton Wanderers in the previous season's FA Cup Final when they famously lost 4-3 to Blackpool in what had become known as the Stanley Matthews final, despite Blackpool's 'other Stan', Mortensen scoring a hat-trick. Langton would certainly provide a lot of goals for centre-forward Tommy Briggs as Blackburn settled into a new pattern of play. Close ties were maintained with Manchester United of course, and a couple of months after leaving Old Trafford, Johnny was back playing in the Tom Curry benefit match against the Scottish side Hibernian. Curry, affectionately known as 'Tosh' to the Manchester United footballers, was a first-rate trainer who in the form of the 1948 team and the Busby Babes would help two of the great Manchester United sides develop and succeed. Johnny certainly proved that he was still a marvellous footballer by slotting into the 1953 Manchester United side as they drew 2-2 against an accomplished Hibernian team. A tragic note to Tom Curry is that he would die alongside his colleagues as a victim of the Munich Air Disaster in 1958.

Back at Ewood Park, the signing of Bobby Langton was having a positive impact with Tommy Briggs going on to score 32 goals from his 40 games that season. Four of these goals would come in the return against Lincoln City who were beaten 6-0 in their visit to Ewood Park, although that still could not erase the memory of that earlier match which is still in the record books 65 years on.

The results Blackburn Rovers obtained put them firmly into the promotion race, which after finishing just ninth in the previous season was a vast improvement. Indeed, until the very last game of the season, Blackburn Rovers would be in the promotion position. Promotion was not to be though, Everton had a vital game in hand which they duly won at relegated Oldham Athletic to secure that second promotion spot behind champions Leicester City.

To strengthen his squad for the following season, Johnny returned to his roots, signing four young Irishman he had seen play in the All Ireland under 18 final between Tower Rovers and Home Farm earlier in the year. One of them, Mick McGrath would become a great player for both Blackburn Rovers and the Republic of Ireland. The young players travelled together over to Blackburn and as Mick recalled: *'Johnny Carey had taken over at Blackburn the season before and already had Ronnie Clayton and Bryan Douglas in his team and, eventually, he would have enough young players for us all to be christened 'Carey's Chicks' in relation to the 'Busby Babes' over at his old club Manchester United. Johnny informed us we would be on £9 a week and quickly informed us of what we could and could not do. The overriding memory was that we always had to show respect.'*

Despite the signings, the 1954-55 season certainly did not get off to the start anybody connected with the Rovers hoped for, as they were well beaten 5-1 at Fulham. That season would be notable for the number of goals Blackburn would score, sadly, they also conceded far too many and slipped down the league to finish in sixth position.

> ### The role of the football manager
>
> When Johnny Carey was appointed manager of Blackburn Rovers in 1953 he brought with him the experience of working under Sir Matt Busby – indisputably one of the greatest managers the game has ever seen. Sir Matt had placed an indelible stamp on Manchester United and shaped the club in his own image. A legacy which lasts to this day. In doing so he rewrote the role of the football manager.
>
> Before the second world war the position of football manager was very different to the role today. Effectively football clubs were under the iron rule of their all-powerful directors. The discretion of managers to buy and sell the players they wanted or appoint and shape coaching staff was very limited. Indeed, when then United manager Scott Duncan left for Ipswich Town in November 1937, a new manager was not recruited and the position was filled for a second time by Club Secretary Walter Crickmer. Crickmer, one of United's great stalwarts, combined the two duties of secretary and manager until the appointment of Busby in October 1945.
>
> Despite no professional managerial experience, the far-sighted Busby demanded unheard-of powers if he was to become United's manager. He would take the job only if he could preside over the appointment of coaches and scouts, the buying and selling of players, and tactics and training. At the behest of Louis Rocca, who was convinced he'd found the right man for the job, United's Chairman James Gibson was happy to oblige. The wisdom of that decision needs no explanation.
>
> At the time, international managers had even less influence over their teams than their club counterparts. England first appointed an official manager (Walter Winterbottom) in 1946, while Scotland continued to manage by committee until Andy Beattie was appointed on a part-time basis in 1954. Squads continued to be selected by committee, and the manager's job was to prepare the players on match day for the task at hand. The 1958 World Cup saw all four of the Home Nations qualify for the finals in Sweden with the following managers: Walter Winterbottom (England); Jimmy Murphy (Wales); Peter Doherty (N Ireland) and Dawson Walker (Scotland, deputising for a recovering Matt Busby). All four squads were selected by committee, and so the managers' ability to mould the team in the way they wanted was minimal. Just as Sir Matt Busby changed the role of club manager, Sir Alf Ramsey was to do the same for international management. Sir Alf's 'wingless wonders' winning the 1966 World Cup shortly after his appointment.

Eddie Quigley was one player that had embraced Johnny's philosophy by then, scoring 28 goals from his 40 matches including a hat-trick in the club's record-breaking 9-0 victory over Middlesbrough at Ewood Park. This is still Blackburn Rover's highest league victory and provides a happier record for Rovers fans than the previous season's disaster at Lincoln City! Frank Mooney also scored a hat-trick in the Middlesbrough game, but, surprisingly, the leading goal scorer Tommy Briggs did not get any. Tommy though, again easily cleared 30 goals, and in the match against Bristol Rovers he scored an incredible seven individual goals in Blackburn's 8-3 victory.

In total that season, Blackburn Rovers would score 114 goals, but they conceded 79 and that poor defensive record put a stop to any promotion hopes. There was still visible progress about the club though, with the younger players such as Clayton and Douglas now in the first team. Mick McGrath was now in the Central League side playing with such developing talents as Peter Dobing and Roy Vernon. 'Carey's Chicks' were now bringing a real feeling that exciting times lay ahead and with the experience of Bill Eckersley, Eddie Crossan, Bobby Langton and Eddie Quigley, the team could also sense success. Johnny, still the quiet-spoken, pipe-smoking, calm man, was their leader as Blackburn Rovers played some of the most beautiful football seen by a Blackburn Rovers side.

Though he was no longer playing, Johnny found the honours still rolling his way. In 1954, he was given the accolade of being in the 100 Football League Legends. Let nobody be surprised, as he would have taken some beating to not be right at the top of that list.

Despite the fall to sixth position, the Blackburn Rovers board and supporters were confident that they had the right man and it was surely only a matter of time before the dream of promotion back to the First Division would be fulfilled.

In the 1955-56 and 1956-57 season, fourth place would be achieved which seemed to put a hold on the high hopes of all at Blackburn.

Johnny had made another playing appearance at his old ground at the end of the 1955-56 championship-winning season for Manchester United as the Busby Babes won what would be the first of two successive league titles. His old friend and full-back partner for many years, Johnny Aston was given a well-deserved testimonial by Manchester United and the newly crowned champions played against an All-Star Xl which, of course, Johnny captained. Johnny Aston's career had ended suddenly due to TB and over 40,000 paid their respects to a great Manchester United player. The All-Star Xl included such as Frank Swift, Tommy Docherty, Henry Cockburn, Tom Finney, Johnny Morris, Nat Lofthouse, Stan Pearson and Jack Rowley, with Johnny settling into the centre-half position. Amongst the other top players who came along to make the All-Stars squad were John Charles, Billy Wright and Bill Eckersley, the Blackburn Rovers full-back and, of course, one of Johnny's players. He must have gone back to Ewood Park still marvelling at the skills of his boss who, even at the age of 37 handled the brilliant forward line of Manchester United without looking out of place. An excellent match would finish 2-1 to the new champions but the All-Star Xl showed why they had that title by playing like the true stars they were.

1957-58 SEASON

At Blackburn Rovers, the younger players were now making the breakthrough. Mick McGrath, Peter Dobing and Roy Vernon were first team regulars by the start of the 1957-58 season and they were joined by a couple of astute signings in Ally MacLeod a flying left-winger brought from Scotland to replace Bobby Langton, and Matt Woods a no-nonsense centre-half to solve any remaining defensive weaknesses. 1957-58 was to be the season that all Johnny's plans and high hopes would be delivered…

It would undoubtedly be one of Blackburn Rover's most exciting seasons, at one point even offering a possible double of League and FA Cup glory, which of course, Johnny had been all too familiar with from his Old Trafford days.

The start of the season did not offer the results hoped for at Ewood Park, with just a single win from the first five matches. Victories followed though, and the flow of goals lifted hopes before inconsistency and defeats brought those hopes back down to earth again. Surely this had to be the year for all of Johnny's planning to come to fruition?

A hat-trick from the flying Scottish left-winger Ally MacLeod against Notts County over Christmas 1957 set the team off on a winning run which not even the loss of form of regular centre-forward Tommy Briggs could stop. To cover the loss of goals from Tommy Briggs, Johnny bought an immediate like for like replacement in Leyton Orient's Tommy Johnston. Johnston quickly hit the goal trail, and with Roy Vernon, Peter Dobing and Bryan Douglas all hitting hat-tricks in various matches, Blackburn Rovers were right in the shake-up as the critical closing matches of the season came around.

Four teams were in that shake-up including three London sides, West Ham United, Fulham and Charlton Athletic, and when Blackburn beat Fulham with only one game to play, that left just three fighting for two places. It meant a shootout between Charlton Athletic and Blackburn as these two were due to meet at The Valley which meant West Ham United were virtually up.

CHARLTON… VICTIMS OF THE CAREY CULT

Charlton 3, Blackburn 4

FOOTBALL'S youngest director, 20-year-old flame-haired Michael Gliksten, of Charlton, spoke the truest and bravest words of the season in his dejected team's dressing - room when he nudged my champagne-sipping arm and said: "Any team that can beat us on our own ground in such a one goal *(writes PETER LORENZO)*. of the Charlton dressing-room to the jubilance of Blackburn's. More champagne (big-heartedly supplied by Charlton) … but this time, there's no bitterness in the bubbles.

Tom Johnston, the £15,000 leader who only once figured in a losing Rovers' side since leaving Orient on March 7, points an arm to his cheroot-smoking team-mates and smiles: "This is going to be the cleverest attack in the First Division next season—if I can keep up with them!"

And 43-goal Johnston—he broke the little toe of his left foot last

Figure 25 'The Carey Cult'

The Valley was a cavernous arena and over 56,000 were present to see which side would get the vital two points to put them into the First Division. A fantastic match saw Charlton score very early, miss a sitter and then see Blackburn Rovers turn on the style and lead 4-1 by the 65th minute! Charlton Athletic now had to go for broke, and go for broke they did, as Blackburn showed signs of really cracking under the extreme pressure as Charlton scored two goals to leave them one point off promotion themselves. Johnny though had the satisfaction of seeing his five-year plan come to fruition, as the final whistle brought the 4-3 victory that put Blackburn in second place, a point behind champions West Ham United and, vitally, a point in front of Charlton Athletic.

The League drama, however, was only a part of Johnny's incredible 1957-58 season as the FA Cup gave real hope of a 'double' while over in Munich, Germany, on 6 February 1958 a real disaster would have a lasting effect on Johnny and his old club Manchester United…

THE MUNICH AIR DISASTER

Matt Busby had asked Johnny to look at his son, Sandy, as a prospective footballer. Matt felt it would be perhaps seen as nepotism to have Sandy playing at Old Trafford, so Johnny gave him a chance as a wing-half at Ewood Park. Sandy was making his way up the football ladder playing for the Rovers' Central League side, when on Thursday 6 February 1958 he finished training and caught his usual train to Manchester before getting the bus to the Busby family home on Kings Road. Sandy recalled what met him in Manchester. *'I saw the billboards at Victoria Station talking about United in a plane crash but thought it was a publicity stunt to get people to buy more papers. Even so I thought I had better give home a call. The answer I got was "Get home quick, get a taxi." When I arrived home the whole house was in a state of shock until we got a phone call to say my dad was alive.'*

Back over in Blackburn, Johnny had just finished an afternoon round of golf when he was told of the disaster. He straight away travelled over to Matt Busby's house to see what, if any, help he could give. One of his tasks was to go on the local television news station in Manchester and try to reassure people of the situation. Once the enormity of the tragedy unfolded, the whole country, indeed world, was shocked at the devastation of a truly great football team, a team Johnny had seen blossoming in his later days at Old Trafford. Johnny was quoted saying, *'I am thinking of my very best friend Matt Busby, and I am sure Manchester United will go on and still be very successful in time.'*

Johnny, obviously, had his duty as Blackburn Rovers manager to fulfil, before that though, in the week after the crash he flew to Munich to be with the survivors, players such as Johnny Berry, Dennis Viollet, Albert Scanlon, Jackie Blanchflower and Ray Wood who he had played alongside at Manchester United. Another, the incredible Duncan Edwards was also then a survivor, before, tragically, he lost his fight for life the week after.

1958 FA CUP RUN

Blackburn Rovers had been very successful in the early years of the FA Cup, with the last of their six successes in 1928 when they had defeated Huddersfield Town 3-1 at Wembley Stadium. Under Johnny they had reached the fifth round in 1955-56 but had not threatened further.

Their 1957-58 campaign started with the same match as when Johnny had taken charge for the first time back in 1953, away at Rotherham United, and with the same 4-1 victory. A visit to Everton seemed a test that would show where Blackburn Rovers stood, as Everton, of course, had pipped Rovers to promotion in that same first season for Johnny as manager. Well, the signs were looking good as Rovers achieved an excellent 2-1 victory at Goodison Park. This brought a third successive away tie, this time in Wales, at Cardiff City. That game was played the week after the Munich tragedy and the Rovers earned a 0-0 draw to bring Cardiff to Ewood Park for the replay. Young players Bryan Douglas and Mick McGrath scored the goals to win the tie 2-1 and, finally give Blackburn a home tie in the sixth-round against Liverpool, themselves a Second Division side at the time.

A crowd of over 50,000 responded to the success Rovers were having, both in the league and cup. As was expected, a fierce North West 'derby' was settled by a close margin, with Rovers getting the vital extra goal in a 2-1 victory. This left the four semi-finalists as Second Division Blackburn Rovers and Fulham, alongside First Division Bolton Wanderers and Manchester United, who were making a remarkable recovery, particularly in the FA Cup. The dream tie for Johnny seemed as though it would have to wait for the final as Blackburn drew local neighbours Bolton in the semi-final to be played at Manchester City's Maine Road, a ground Johnny had filled with distinction in those long years Manchester United had to ground share after their bomb-damaged Old Trafford was repaired.

Sadly, there was to be no dream Wembley meeting as Rovers, despite taking the lead through Peter Dobing, lost a thrilling match 2-1 to Bolton when the stand-in for injured Nat Lofthouse, Ralph Gubbins, scored twice inside a minute just before half-time, sending Bolton through to face Manchester United. Bolton would go on to win the final 2-0 against the weight of public sympathy for the stricken Manchester United club, slowly coming to terms with life after their tragic air disaster. Still, for Blackburn Rovers there would be the massive consolation of gaining promotion back to the First Division, led by their quiet, pipe-smoking legend of football, Johnny Carey.

TIME FOR A CHANGE

Back in 1953 when Johnny had taken on the role of Blackburn Rovers manager he decided that he did not want a contract, he would have a gentleman's agreement of a month notice either way for the partnership to be dissolved. Johnny felt that he had a need to have the freedom to stop managing, move on elsewhere, or just continue at Rovers as manager. Compare today where managers get three to five-year contracts, often quickly followed by the sack, and move onto another club with a bumper pay off to start again.

Figure 26 Blackburn Rovers 1958-59

By the start of the 1958-59 season he had finally achieved promotion, had a real go at winning the FA Cup, while in the background he had transformed the production line of young players coming through the system. Indeed, that season Blackburn Rovers would win the FA Youth Cup beating West Ham United over two legs, a competition which for its first five seasons had been the sole possession of Johnny's former club Manchester United. The Blackburn side would feature players such as Keith Newton, Mike England and Fred Pickering, all going on to have excellent careers. England becoming one of the top centre-halves around for both Blackburn and Tottenham Hotspur and as a Welsh international, while Newton would play in the 1970 World Cup for England, and Pickering attracting a large transfer move to Everton.

By the time the Blackburn Rovers youth side would win the FA Youth Cup though, Johnny Carey would no longer be with the Rovers...

BLACKBURN ROVERS AUGUST TO OCTOBER 1958

For their first match back in the First Division since 1948, Rovers travelled to the North East to play Newcastle United. This brought a reunion of two of the stars of Manchester United's famous FA Cup-winning side of 1948, this time as opposition managers, Johnny in charge of Blackburn Rovers and Charlie Mitten in charge of Newcastle United. Charlie, of course, a man who had been involved in that sensational transfer to Columbia during United's tour of America in 1950.

Such meetings with old teammates were rare though, and of the Manchester United 1948 FA Cup winners who went into management, Johnny always looked the stand out one to succeed as a boss. And, so it would prove. Allenby Chilton did get Grimsby Town into the Second Division but could not keep them there, Jack Rowley had his time at Plymouth Argyle, while Charlie Mitten had some success at Newcastle United, although he would see them relegated the next season.

It would be Johnny who would have the larger grin after this match as his newly promoted side turned in a marvellous display winning 5-1 against a Newcastle side that contained such as former Portsmouth star Jimmy Scoular, that brilliant ball player George Eastham and an exquisite winger in Bobby Mitchell. The Rovers side themselves were now a finely balanced combination of talent brought through the club and experienced professionals. The team that took the field at St. James's Park for this opening encounter was: Leyland; Whelan; Eckersley; Clayton; Woods; McGrath; Douglas; Dobing; Johnston; Vernon and McLeod.

An unchanged side faced Leicester City at Ewood Park mid-week and went one better by not conceding a goal but scoring five again! They waited until the 65th minute for the first goal but then ran riot. When the same score was repeated on the Saturday at home to Tottenham Hotspur, Johnny was indeed back in the big time in style. His team now fashioned in his own image displayed all of his attributes of skill, thoughtful passing and excellent defending. A 1-1 draw away at Leicester in mid-week set Johnny up for an emotional return to Old Trafford to face a Manchester United side bravely rebuilding after the Munich air disaster of seven months ago.

The first return to Old Trafford for Johnny as a manager brought a crowd of 65,187 to see a match between two sides right at the top of the table, Rovers in fact, with seven points from a possible eight. Manchester United fielding players such as Bobby Charlton, Dennis Viollet, Harry Gregg, Billy Foulkes and Albert Scanlon who had all played in that fateful last match in Belgrade seven months ago to the day. Sadly, for Blackburn, Rovers found United in irresistible form as they stormed to a 6-1 victory with both Charlton and Viollet scoring two each, along with goals from Alex Dawson and Albert Scanlon, with Tommy Johnston scoring Rover's consolation. After the match Matt Busby recalled how Johnny accepted the result with his usual Irish humour and was heard to quietly remark as he studied the results in the boardroom after the game; *'There are some funny results today!'*

One of those funny results was from across Lancashire in the city of Liverpool as Everton lost their fifth successive match, at home to Arsenal by the same score as over at Old Trafford 6-1. They would soon want somebody to stop this almighty slump, and the man they set their eyes on was to be

Johnny over at Blackburn Rovers. Johnny, of course, was in the position of only being on a month's notice either way. Blackburn must have felt reasonably comfortable that after five years on such an agreement, and with a side that was settling into the First Division he would be content to stay. Everton were a sleeping giant though, playing at a stadium, Goodison Park, which could hold over 70,000 passionate supporters.

By mid-September the call that had been expected came through from Everton chairman Mr R. E. Searle to Blackburn Rovers chairman Mr G. N. Forbes, asking permission to speak to Johnny. How would Johnny respond? Well, Blackburn did not give in without prolonged discussion, offering to match the alleged salary offer of £3,000 per year, but the lure of such a big club with a contract reputedly for five years, was too big for Johnny to turn down. In a typically mature manner Johnny did not just down tools at Ewood Park but stayed for the month he had agreed to in his contract with Rovers, which allowed them to appoint Dally Duncan the Luton Town manager as his replacement, giving him the time to settle in at Blackburn.

Johnny told Roy Cavanagh of his days at Blackburn Rovers. *They were very enjoyable times at Ewood Park, lovely people in charge and excellent players such as Bryan Douglas who I rated very highly indeed. It was very sad to leave but Everton came along with an offer I could not turn down, especially as I had a family to look after. On my departure I stressed to the club not to let the team break up as they could be a very successful team.'*

The words of his wife Margaret Carey sum up the Carey time at Blackburn Rovers; *'Jack had become manager at Blackburn Rovers in July 1953, during that time we lost a baby son and also my father, but we had some very happy times, the happiest being when Rovers were promoted to the First Division. The secretary at Rovers was then Reg Taylor, a wonderful secretary he was too, and we had some marvellous times with him and his wife Dolly. Jack and I liked living in Blackburn. In spite of what many people think, it is a fine place, with warm people, lovely countryside on the doorstep and the seaside easily reached. Jack had several offers to manage other clubs and as he did not have a contract with Rovers he was free to go. However, the temptation was too much when Everton offered the position. He had always admired the club, it wasn't too far from our friends and the money was very good-also a five-year contract.'*

Johnny could move on to the next chapter of his life with his head held high. In his five years at Blackburn he had lifted the team from ninth place in the Second Division into a promising position in the First Division. In doing so, transforming the club from an experienced, but ageing team, into one with youthful flair in the first team and the promise of much more to come from the firm foundations of their youth system. Would he be able to achieve the same success at Everton?

Chapter Ten

TAXI FOR...

Johnny Carey was a man of his word. Everton had to wait a month after their official approach made on the 22nd September 1958 for Johnny to work his notice at Blackburn Rovers. That month at Everton was eventful. They lost disastrously 10-4 at Tottenham Hotspur, in a match that saw Bill Nicholson take charge of his first match as Tottenham manager. Then, the following week, Everton beat Manchester United 3-2 at Goodison Park in a game that saw the strange situation of neither side having a manager in charge! Obviously, Everton were still waiting for Johnny to take up his role, while for Manchester United, both their manager Matt Busby and assistant Jimmy Murphy were opposing each other in a Wales v Scotland international match. Despite their victory, Everton were still second from bottom of the table.

Meanwhile Johnny and his family moved into the lovely area of Birkdale. Their house was close to the beach, and his children settled quickly into their new schools. Birkdale is home to a famous Golf Club, where Johnny would enjoy playing off a handicap of four.

The appointment of Johnny as a manager marked a change of direction for Everton. Back in 1956, following the departure of Cliff Britton, the club announced that its directors would never appoint a manager again. Ian Buchan had been the chief coach since then, but the poor start the side had made in the 1958-59 season forced a complete change of plan for the club. After just 13 matches they had conceded 40 goals. There were some decent players at Goodison Park though, Scottish international Bobby Collins had joined from Glasgow Celtic and Alex Parker from Falkirk at the start of this season, and this gave Johnny something to build on.

That was the theme of Johnny's first message to Evertonians via the Liverpool Daily Post on 21 October 1958. Below the headline *'Carry on Everton!'* the article informed fans that *'Under new management the club may be, but Mr Johnny Carey's first orders were; "Away with the brooms. There will be no clean-sweep here".'* Indeed, Johnny also said, *'Things are even better than I expected. It's a wonderful club-I've always known that-but you have to see things from the inside to appreciate just how wonderful. The greatness and traditions of Everton is not only on the surface- it permeates the club.'*

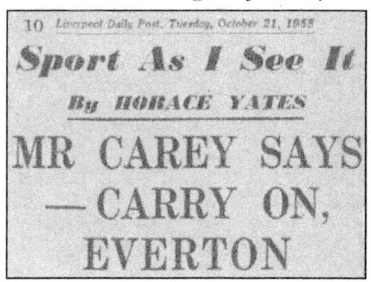

Figure 27 'Carry on Everton'

Johnny was true to his word, as he made no signings in the rest of his first season. He steadied the Everton side instantly, as they went undefeated in his first four matches, which included a quick meeting with his previous team, Blackburn Rovers that ended in a 2-2 draw. One thing Johnny was not happy about though was the state of the Goodison Park pitch which he felt would not suit the type of football he wanted the side to play. So concerned was he with the pitch that early in his tenure he even moved an FA Youth Cup match, ironically against his former club Manchester United, across Stanley Park to be played at Anfield.

Everton finished in 16th position in the 1958-59 season, up from 21st when Johnny had arrived. In the FA Cup, after beating Sunderland and Charlton Athletic (after a replay), they suffered a heavy 4-1 defeat at home to Aston Villa. Everton were firm favourites for this tie, but a former star of Goodison Park, Joe Mercer, was the Villa manager and he had them fully prepared. Johnny knew, that while he had not yet made changes, new players would be needed in vital areas to complement the likes of Bobby Collins and Alex Parker.

Bobby Collins was a tremendous inside-forward who had played against Johnny in his last official match for Manchester United, the Coronation Cup tie against Glasgow Celtic. He very quickly recognised the impact Johnny would have at Everton, saying about his new manager *'He had a wealth of experience, a great tactician, he gave you a job, and it was down to the player to make sure it worked.'*

Johnny's first season had shown progress, and at the start of the 1959-60 season, there was much optimism that further improvement would be made. In a worrying reminder of the previous season's start though, the side had to wait until the seventh match of the season to gain their first win, ironically against Blackburn Rovers at Goodison Park by 2-0. Three games soon after, summed up the unpredictability of Everton at the time. A 6-1 home win against Leicester City was followed by an 8-2 hammering away at Newcastle United, which must have been particularly hard for Johnny as his old teammate Charlie Mitten was still at Newcastle as manager. Then, returning to Goodison Park, Everton defeated Birmingham City 4-0. A difficult start to 1960 came with a 2-0 defeat away in the 3rd round of the FA Cup to Third Division Bradford City. This was probably the final straw for Johnny, who went to the board for the money that he would need to transform his side.

The club backed their manager. Winger Tommy Ring joined Everton from Scottish side Clyde in January, then between mid-February and early March, two top players who would go on to have brilliant careers with Everton were signed. Firstly, inside-left Roy Vernon, a man who Johnny had nurtured at Blackburn Rovers arrived at Goodison Park for a fee of £27,000. The expectant 51,000 crowd that saw his debut were disappointed as would be champions Wolverhampton Wanderers won 2-0. Next, that hard-tackling wing-half Jimmy Gabriel came south from Dundee, making his debut in a 2-2 draw away at West Ham United, with Vernon getting both Everton goals.

Roy Vernon was a character. He had the habit of smoking in the communal bath, and when some of his teammates pushed his head under the water, he would still come up with the cigarette in his mouth! He must have been able to put it inside his mouth. He was a character on the pitch too, where he was a creative inside-left and a goal scorer. A Welsh international he had been part of the team that reached the 1958 World Cup quarter-finals against Brazil, narrowly losing 1-0 to a Pele goal.

The new signings soon settled in, with Everton going on a six-game undefeated run at the end of the season, spoilt somewhat by a heavy 5-0 defeat at Old Trafford against Manchester United in the last game. This left Everton in the same 16th position as the season before. The knowledgeable Goodison Park faithful though had seen signs of improvement, not least through the arrival of Vernon and Gabriel, and the emergence of centre-half Brian Labone alongside the still excellent Collins and Parker. The news that millionaire John Moores, owner of the Littlewoods empire, would take over as chairman for the 1960-61 season from Dick Searle gave fans hope that the corner would be turned, and Everton would once again be one of England's finest sides. Their hopes would come true, but with a nasty surprise at the end of it for Johnny Carey…

SEASON 1960-61

John Moores was an extremely wealthy man, used to getting things done quickly he would not want to be a patient man. The previous season, despite the arrival of Johnny, had seen the side fail to produce the required form and results. The club had a laudable policy of building and training local talent, but relegation was again a possibility, so a change of policy was made by entering the transfer market, backed by John Moores' wealth. The signings of Roy Vernon and Jimmy Gabriel had improved the team, and there was no doubt that further incomings were likely. In his first comments to the fans, John Moores stated that *'Rome had not been built in a day and he expected that the team would do well in the coming season.'*

Also on the Everton board was the son of the legendary Jack Sharp, one of the finest sportsmen England has ever seen. His son, also named Jack Sharp, was now a wealthy businessman with a thriving sports business in Liverpool. Jack Sharp senior is one of only 12 men to have played full internationals for England at both football AND cricket. He also won the FA Cup with Everton and the County Cricket Championship with Lancashire. A fellow team-mate, Harry Makepeace, remains the only man to complete the full set of having played both football and cricket for England and won the Football League, FA Cup and County Cricket Championship.

Everton Football Club Co. Ltd.
(Founded 1878)

CUP FINAL No. 1 VOUCHER

Chairman: JOHN MOORES

Directors:
R. E. SEARLE J. C. SHARP N. W. COFFEY
C. E. BALMFORTH F. MICKLESFIELD J. TAYLOR
R. A. JOYNSON E. HOLLAND HUGHES

Manager: J. J. CAREY *Secretary:* W. DICKINSON

EVERTONIA

The Chairman, Directors, Management and Staff, at the commencement of another new season, offer a cordial welcome to all Supporters of the Club and hope, with you, that many good matches will be witnessed in our stadium, and that the end of the season will see us amongst honours winners.

Our new Chairman gives below his appreciation of the hopes for the new season.

The opening of the 1960-61 Season at Goodison Park finds us in the midst of a tremendous effort to build a side worthy of the Everton tradition.

In January, 1960, the Club's position was a desperate one and it seemed we were heading for relegation, so the Directors decided for the moment to put aside the policy of producing and training local talent, and enter the transfer market. To obtain experienced and talented players is easier said than done, but by paying heavily we were able to sign several very fine players.

The standard of our play improved immediately, we began to attract good crowds again, and we made our position in the League safe. But we still weren't really in the top class. Perhaps our new players hadn't settled down perfectly, or perhaps the tense struggle for League points prevented us obtaining that perfect blend which produces the outstanding side.

Mr. John Moores

The Directors, Manager, Coaches and Players all feel we have the making of a really first-class team. The pre-season training has given our Manager, Johnny Carey, the opportunity of moulding the players into a well-knit unit.

Give them your wholehearted support and encourage them as much as you possibly can by letting them feel you are with them all the way. They will need all the encouragement you can give, for it would have been difficult to have chosen a more severe opening programme. Of our first four matches we are due to play Spurs away, and Manchester United at home and away—what a blooding for a newly constituted team.

Just as Rome wasn't built in a day, Everton won't be re-built in the first few weeks of the season, but I'm quietly confident we will do well in 1960-61, when I hope and believe we will be able to give you something to enthuse about. Time and experience will show if and where we need to be further strengthened, but I do assure you the Directors will leave no stone unturned to produce a side which will equal those great Everton sides of the past.

JOHN MOORES, *Chairman.*

Figure 28 John Moores' message to the Everton faithful

This 1960-61 season would prove to be Everton's finest since the war. An opening match away at Tottenham Hotspur was never going to be an easy start, but what nobody knew at the time was that this was a genuinely great Tottenham side. They were leaders from day one and went on to achieve the first League and FA Cup double since Aston Villa in 1897, when incidentally, the elder Jack Sharp, had played for Aston Villa.. Tottenham won the opener 2-0, but the following Wednesday, before a crowd of over 51,000, Everton entertained one of Johnny's former clubs, Manchester United. The Goodison faithful liked what they saw, as Everton won 4-0 with another Carey signing, Micky Lill from Wolverhampton Wanderers scoring two of the goals.

A start of two wins and three defeats left Everton 13th before the team hit form and went on an incredible run of only one defeat in 19 matches. Indeed, but for the sheer pace set by Tottenham Hotspur, Everton would have been fighting for pole position instead of third in the table. Another couple of signings were made. Billy Bingham, the Northern Ireland outside-right signed from Luton Town, and a footballer who still today ranks in the finest Roy Cavanagh has seen, Alex Young, joined from Hearts in Scotland. Young was not a big man, but still played a lot of games in the centre-forward position. In later years he would be known as *The Golden Vision* such was his creativity and goal-scoring ability.

Young's debut came in the return fixture with Tottenham Hotspur at Goodison Park, played in mid-December 1960, when before a crowd of 61,000, Tottenham showed what a great side they were by winning 3-1. Still, as Christmas arrived, Everton were third and playing open, attractive, football, firmly in the mode Johnny had envisaged for his team. The new inside-forward trio of Bobby Collins, Alex Young and Roy Vernon were as good as any around. Then came an unaccountable sequence of seven defeats, which included being knocked out of the FA Cup by Bury, and in the new Football League Cup, defeat by Shrewsbury Town. The five league defeats pushed Everton down to a season-low of fifth, which was still a vast improvement on recent seasons.

A 3-1 away win at Blackburn Rovers at the end of March 1961 preceded a run of six victories and a draw in the last seven matches which kept Everton in fifth position. Johnny's previous clubs Manchester United and Blackburn Rovers were in seventh and eighth spots respectively. Incredibly, Johnny would not be the manager for all of these fixtures as during an infamous taxi-ride in London he was sensationally sacked by chairman John Moores, hence the title of this chapter which is a catchphrase that persists to this day.

The reasons for Johnny's sacking are hard to pin down. Certainly, in mid-January, when the abolition of the maximum wage was announced, Johnny supported the decision while, allegedly, Everton were against it. Then came the seven defeats including embarrassing cup defeats by lower league sides Bury and Shrewsbury. Perhaps crucially, though John Moores heard that

Harry Catterick, who he was friendly with, was making it known that he had gone as far as he could at Sheffield Wednesday, the only side that had given Tottenham Hotspur cause for concern that season.

Whatever the reasons, a few days after Everton had hammered Newcastle United 4-0 away at St James Park, both John Moores and Johnny Carey represented Everton at a Football League meeting at the Café Royal in London. On the journey back to their hotel Johnny asked Moores for clarification of the rumours that were beginning to emerge about his position. At this point, John Moores dropped the bombshell to Johnny in the back of their taxi that he was to be sacked with at least two years still left on his contract. The saying, *'Taxi for'* became part of folklore.

Johnny Carey Visits Goodison Park Today

JOHNNY CAREY, who yesterday lost his £3,000 a year post as manager of Everton F.C., is visiting Goodison Park this afternoon to "collect my things, have a talk with club officials, and watch the First Division game, Everton v. Cardiff City".

Figure 29 A sad farewell

Despite always being such a cool, calm man, this was shattering news to Johnny and his family. All of football was shocked by the dismissal. In an instant comment, Johnny was quoted as saying *'I had been at Everton before Mr Moores arrived and it felt he wanted his own choice as manager, somebody who cracked whips instead of influencing players' minds. That was not my style, and I was out.'* The football world recoiled at what was perceived as a savage dismissal, certainly Matt Busby at Manchester United was disgusted by his former player's sacking, whilst as Johnny took his seat in the Goodison Park stand for the match with Cardiff City the cheers and applause from the Everton faithful made everybody, including the Everton board, aware of their views.

On the Monday after the Cardiff match, which Everton had won 5-1, Harry Catterick was announced as the new Everton manager. He was, of course, a former centre-forward at the club and had guested for Manchester United in the war-years playing alongside Johnny. His record at Sheffield Wednesday had been excellent and, in time, he would go onto become one of Everton's greatest managers winning the League and FA Cup, but who was to say that Johnny had not already put most of the jigsaw together for him?

The following week Johnny instructed his lawyers *'to enforce my rights under my contract with Everton and to clear my name. I should add that I do not know of any reason which would entitle the Everton directors to ask for my resignation.'* It would be February 1962 before the case was settled outside of court.

On Saturday 22 April 1961, for the first time since he was a 17-year-old back in Dublin, Johnny attended a football match as an ordinary spectator as he took in the Preston North End v Manchester United match at Deepdale as a guest of his friend and mentor Matt Busby. Just as the week before at Goodison Park, the ordinary supporter was full of admiration towards him as they applauded, sought autographs or just wanted to shake the hand of 'Gentleman John.'

As we did at the end of his time at Blackburn Rovers, let his wife Margaret give her views on her husband's time at Everton *'After Rovers, we went off to live in Birkdale with stars in our eyes. We found a lovely house and expected to have at least the five years on Jack's contract-we were very innocent in those days! Our daughter Patricia was born there in 1960, the same year that my mother passed away, Jack's father had died in 1959. He and my mother always spent a holiday with us each year, and we were to sorely miss them both. Then in April 1961, millionaire chairman Mr John Moores sacked Jack-quite out of the blue. I shouldn't have been too surprised though, as when he was made chairman in July 1960, I had a hunch he would never understand that people have different ways of getting the best out of people and his was to be tough and my husband's persuasive. However, we were shattered that this happened to Jack, he had been an idol to so many people which makes it harder to take the knocks.'*

Johnny Carey left Everton with his reputation and integrity intact. A man with his experience and ability would be in demand. The question was, which opportunity would he take next. The answer was a surprise to many…

Chapter Eleven

TIME IN THE ORIENT

As soon as the football world knew of Johnny Carey's position, there was no shortage of suitors from across Britain. From one end of the country to the other, from Plymouth Argyle, via Preston North End and Wrexham, all the way to Greenock Morton interest was expressed. Surprisingly perhaps, it was Second Division Leyton Orient and their charismatic chairman Harry Zussman, known as 'The Fairy Godmother', that convinced Johnny and his family to make the move South. Zussman led a colourful board of directors that included showbusiness moguls Lew Grade and Leslie and Bernard Delfont. Bernard Delfont and Lew and Leslie Grade were, in fact, all brothers, Lew and Bernard born in Ukraine, then part of Imperial Russia, and Leslie in London, all with the surname Winogradsky. The brothers changed their names to the ones that became synonymous with the world of show business in 1960s Britain. Their friendship with shoe magnate Harry Zussman led all three to support Leyton Orient in the East End of London.

Johnny's first match in charge of Orient was away at Newcastle United, just four months after his Everton side had inflicted a damaging defeat on them as they had unsuccessfully fought to stave off relegation. This time the result was a goalless draw but became part of a very satisfactory start, consisting of just one defeat from the first seven matches.

Although Leyton Orient had skirted with relegation the previous season, Johnny saw players around him who had talent, including some he had even played with and against. Eddie Lewis had been with Johnny at Manchester United in the period before the Busby Babes, while Bill Robertson was in the Chelsea net the night Johnny's goal effectively sealed the First Division title for United back in 1952. Johnny was quick to remind him of this, jokingly remarking *'I remembered it very well, although I never held it against Bill that he was one of the few goalkeepers I could score against!'*.

Another player with Leyton Orient as Johnny arrived was fan favourite, centre-forward Tommy Johnston. Johnny had signed Tommy from Orient to help push Blackburn Rovers over the promotion line back in 1958. Tommy had returned to Leyton Orient after Johnny left for Everton, but in what was a surprise to many people, Johnny moved Tommy on to Gillingham. It seemed Johnny wanted Tommy, then a 34-year-old, to help bring the reserve players through, but Tommy still wanted his first-team wage of £25. Orient could only afford £17, so a parting of the ways ensued. Such was the esteem that Tommy Johnston was held at Brisbane Road, that in 2008 when he died in Australia, the then Orient chairman Barry Hearn named a stand after him.

Following his more than decent start at Orient, Johnny gave an interview to Sunday Express reporter Alan Hoby reflecting on his recent time at Everton and his present one at Brisbane Road. Alan Hoby firstly wrote about one of the most sensational sackings, even in the restless, *'ulcers-and-aspirin'* world of big-time soccer back in the early 1960's.

Figure 30 The come-back

'Gentleman John' was the most complete footballer Hoby had ever seen, recalling that in his majestic heyday that he played in so many different positions, even a full match in goal. The move from Goodison Park's splendour to the *'homely'* atmosphere of Brisbane Road was, in Hoby's words, *'one of the most amazing managerial somersaults football has seen'*. Johnny exchanging the plush magnificence of famous *'buy anybody Everton'* for a club whose continued existence was a never-ending miracle. A club in Leyton Orient who would have died long ago but for the boundless generosity of its supporters' club and board of directors headed by that jovial optimist, shoe magnate Harry Zussman.

At Everton Johnny had occupied a swank, streamlined office, furnished in the most modern manner. He had his own secretary and had spent nearly £200,000 in his two years at the club, taking them to their highest position since the war with an average crowd of over 43,000. The contrast Johnny found when he turned up in East London, started with no secretary, no office even, no stars on the pitch and no money to bring anybody in, an average crowd of 12,000 and a much-reduced salary.

So, what was Johnny Carey's response to Alan Hoby, *'I have no comment to make about Everton, all I know is that in my own mind I was never a failure. But let us talk about Leyton Orient'* Carey went on with a smile, *'I was in the running for other clubs. Instead, I came to Leyton Orient, and I am delighted I did. It is the sort of club where, as Alex Stock once said when he was manager here; "If you want a cup of tea you simply bang on the wall and shout for it." Yes, there is a terrific surplus of heart and humanity here. As for any feeling that it is some sort of come-down to go from Everton to Leyton Orient such a thought never entered my head. It is a great relief to be where you are really appreciated; where everybody's only too ready to do all they can to help you-as Les Gore the assistant manager who had the team before me and Eddie Baily our coach have done.'*

Hoby then reflected on the way Johnny had made subtle changes already at Brisbane Road, the controversial transfer of leading scorer Tommy Johnston and two other moves bringing from Wrexham two young wing halves, Hal Lucas and Cyril Lea. Johnny replied, *'They have both done well- although there is a long way to go yet.'* Typically understated, a mark of Johnny, both as one of the world's greatest footballers and now as a manager.

> ### The Showbiz Club
>
> *Leyton Orient were initially named Clapton Orient from their location in the East End of London, at the heart of the Jewish community. Despite their relocation to Leyton, the club retained much of its Jewish support and Jewish shoe magnate, Harry Zussman was elected chairman of Leyton Orient in 1949 after the death of the previous chairman George Harris. Known to many as London's Cinderella team due to their lack of success, under the stewardship of Zussman the club began to improve, and in 1956, they were promoted from Division Three (South) to Division Two for the first time in their history.*
>
> *In 1959, Zussman brought three of his social acquaintances into the club in the form of brothers, Bernard Delfont and Lew and Leslie Grade. The three brothers dominated the entertainment scene in the UK in those days, and so Orient quickly became known as the 'Showbiz Club' with many famous stars now visiting the club. Together with Zussman, the brothers provide a remarkable rags-to-riches story of East End entrepreneurs done good, that would have perhaps been too fanciful for one of their own stage or screen productions. Bernard and Lew were born in Ukraine in the early 1900s, then part of the Russian Empire. With Leslie, they were the three sons of Isaak and Olga Winogradsky. The family emigrated to escape Cossack violence and anti-Semitism via Berlin to Brick Lane in Bethnal Green in the East End of London, where Leslie, youngest of the three brothers was born. While their parents worked in textiles, all three brothers went on to work in showbusiness changing their names in the process. Bernard Delfont entered theatrical management after careers as first a dancer, then an agent. He presented over 200 shows in London and New York City. Lew Grade had also started out as a dancer, but together with the youngest of the brothers, Leslie became two of the UK's best-known and most respected media executives, playing a crucial part in the development of British television.*
>
> *Their presence at the club firmly put Orient onto the footballing map as the club too followed a rags-to-riches trajectory. With promotion to the First Division in 1962, Orient, who had been known as the Cinderella Club, completed one of football's great fairy tales.*

Although a couple of results went against them, a belief was starting to develop that this Orient side were going places. The belief was strengthened when Johnny returned to Merseyside to take on Liverpool, themselves then in the Second Division under the managership of the legendary Bill Shankly and achieved a 3-3 draw before a crowd of over 36,000. David Dunmore getting two of the Orient goals and Roger Hunt doing likewise for Liverpool. Liverpool were undoubtedly going places, and Bill Shankly had recruited well with such as Ian St John and Ron Yeats arriving from Scotland, Gordon Milne from Preston North End, all joining players that had already come through the Liverpool ranks like Roger Hunt, Ronnie Moran, Ged Byrne, Alan A'Court and Jimmy Melia.

Orient's results then seemed to match Johnny Carey's Everton's games of a year before. A run of 14 undefeated, which included an excellent 1-1 draw away at the then First Division league leaders Burnley in the FA Cup, was followed by a series of five defeats, including the replay defeat against Burnley, 1-0 at Brisbane Road.

Possibly the turning point came in two matches against Stoke City and Sunderland as the season took shape in February and March. Stoke City had attempted to address a slump in form and brought back Stanley Matthews from Blackpool and signed Dennis Viollet from Manchester United. These two would eventually take Stoke City back to the First Division, but not this season, as Leyton Orient won 1-0 at the Victoria Ground to put an end to their own poor run. The week after, a 1-1 home draw with Sunderland, and their inspired forward Brian Clough, would prove crucial at the end of the season. That end of season run-in would see only one defeat in the last ten games, ending with a nerve-racking final day.

On the last day of the season a revitalised Liverpool were well and truly over the hill, eight points clear of Orient and already promoted. With one promotion spot remaining Sunderland were level on points with Leyton Orient but with a better goal difference. They would be away at Swansea Town (they changed from Town to City in 1969) while Leyton Orient were at home to Bury.

As a prelude to the match, Leyton Orient Chairman Harry Zussman contacted the Swansea Town manager, Trevor Morris, and suggested that any positive result would be rewarded by the finest hat that money could buy. Trevor Morris felt any such achievement against Sunderland would be worth more than a hat and suggested Zussman bought him a fine suit!

On that final day, an expectant crowd filled Brisbane Road, with the players having the dubious pleasure of a visit from a top comedian of the time Arthur Askey in the dressing room before the match. The crowd erupted when they saw Malcolm Graham glide a header into the Bury net after five minutes. At half-time news filtered through that Sunderland were 1-0 up at Swansea thanks to a Brian Clough goal and heading for the First Division. Coincidentally, Bury were being led brilliantly defensively by their centre-half Bob Stokoe, who would, of course, become a Sunderland legend in later years. As news came through halfway through the second-half that Swansea had equalised, the Orient fans went wild with delight. Their celebrations increased when Malcolm Graham scored his second with five minutes to go and sealed an incredible promotion for one of football's 'Cinderella' clubs, Leyton Orient. The crowd's chants of *'We want Carey, we want Carey'* echoed around the packed Brisbane Road ground on a day of one of football's greatest fairy tales. The Leyton Orient team on this historic day was: Robertson; Charlton (capt); Lewis; Lucas; Bishop; Lea; Deeley; Gibbs; Dunmore; Graham and McDonald.

As an after-match note, while chairman Harry Zussman was busily ringing his West End tailor to arrange an excellent suit for Trevor Morris over at Swansea Town, Orient director Bernard Delfont came into the ecstatic dressing room and asked goal scoring hero Malcolm Graham to choose whatever he wanted. Graham, not thinking, asked for a bottle of champagne, wishing in later years that he had asked for the rented clubhouse he was living in, convinced Delfont would have given it to him!

Figure 31 Malcolm Graham celebrates promotion

There was a pleasing symmetry in Leyton Orient's results this season, the 21 home and 21 away matches each produced 11 victories, 5 draws and 5 defeats. So, one spring morning in April 1962 the citizens of East London woke to find another First Division side in their manor besides West Ham United. Leyton Orient, a humble club of slender resources but considerable ambition, had played fast, flowing football all season and had finally won a season-long struggle with Sunderland to accompany Liverpool in leaving the Second Division behind.

Seventy-five miles away from Orient's ground, another homely, small football club, Ipswich Town had just completed their incredible rise from lower league to winning the First Division Championship. Surely it could not happen again, this time with Leyton Orient?

1962-63 SEASON

Once Leyton Orient's 'dream' season in the First Division started, with a home game against Arsenal, it soon became apparent that the ground would be full, part of the increase in support being the many show business friends of Lew and Leslie Grade and Bernard Delfont! The team though, were the ones in the first two months who had the locals buzzing, as they won famous victories over Everton, Manchester United and two London sides, West Ham United and Fulham.

August had not started well with three defeats, including 2-1 to Arsenal on the opening day, and one draw. But, by the end of September, Leyton Orient had those four victories and a draw, and despite three further defeats they were in 12th position with teams such as Manchester United, Manchester City, Arsenal and the previous champions Ipswich Town below them in the League table.

The matches with Everton home and away were separated by the visit of Manchester United to Brisbane Road. All three would, of course, be emotional for Johnny and the Goodison Park crowd of over 51,000 gave him a marvellous reception on his return to Everton. The home side were already in fine form and won 3-0, but even so, Orient gave them a tough match. Although obviously disappointed with the result, Johnny Carey must have taken some consolation from the fact that all three Everton goals were scored by players he had signed for Everton - Billy Bingham, Jimmy Gabriel and Roy Vernon.

When Manchester United rolled into Brisbane Road in early September, they paraded their £115,000 summer signing from Italy, Denis Law. So far this season, Law had not been joined by Bobby Charlton who was still suffering from an injury, but they had already won in London at Arsenal and United would provide a real test for Orient. The match brought all the main reporters to Brisbane Road covering the story of the link between the two managers Matt Busby and Johnny Carey. One of those reporters was a man of many talents, Clement Freud who covered the match for The Observer. His coverage started thus:

Figure 32 Match Programme, Orient v United

'*With a minute to go before the final whistle, Leyton Orient scored a goal that turned a well-deserved moral victory into an actual one and showed that their prior inferiority of position was due to lack of fortune rather than to any shortage of talent or application. The scorer was McDonald, a crew cut left-winger who had done nothing previously to suggest the glory would be his. Picking up an Eddie Lewis clearance he set off inside as opposed to outside before blasting a shot which flew past David Gaskell in the United goal. United gave little, Denis Law was helping his full-backs more than worrying Bill Robertson in the Orient goal.*'

Johnny must have sat back with satisfaction at achieving a victory for such a small club against one of the biggest clubs in the game, a club he had helped achieve that fame. Strolling, pipe in mouth down to the dressing rooms, the first man he saw was the diminutive Manchester United Chairman Harold Hardman, who stopped to congratulate Johnny on a fine victory. Another famous victory would be only days away for Johnny, this time one with a real feeling for him, as his side beat the top of the table, Everton, gaining revenge not just on the week previous, but Johnny must also have felt, for his unjust dismissal from that club, 17 months ago.

'*Once again, unfashionable Leyton Orient proved to be the big occasion team, having just beaten Manchester United, you will pardon me if I don't drag up the old cliché, but Orient played this one for Johnny.*' reported the Daily Mirror as Orient amazed all of the football world by thoroughly outplaying Everton and winning 3-0.

Two goals early in the second-half from winger Norman Deeley and inside-right Gordon Bolland sent the 21,756 fans wild and when David Dunmore scored a third late on it matched the score from the previous week. Dunmore was a top-class centre-forward who Johnny Carey was amazed never played for England. Everton would go on to win the First Division that season, two years after Johnny Carey had left so ignominiously. They did so with at least nine players who had played first-team football for Johnny on their playing staff, including such vital signings as Alex Young, Roy Vernon, Jimmy Gabriel and Billy Bingham.

When his team travelled from East to West London and beat Fulham 2-0 at the end of September, Johnny must have been on top of the world. Little, unfancied, Leyton Orient were in 12th place in the First Division. It wasn't to last though, and Orient would not win again in the First Division until April, although they recorded victories in both the Football League and FA Cup.

In the Football League Cup, Orient did get to the 5th round before a surprise 2-0 loss to Second Division Bury at Brisbane Road, the same side they had beat 2-0 the previous April to gain promotion. In this run, Orient had beat Chester City 9-2 at home. The FA Cup also saw Orient reach the 5th round to meet high flying Leicester City, who won 1-0 at Brisbane Road. Leicester would reach the 1963 final, losing to Johnny Carey's old club Manchester United 3-1, United's first triumph since the Munich Air Disaster in 1958.

There was another consideration to add to this story of Leyton Orient. From Boxing Day 1962 until late February 1963 football became a casualty of one of Britain's worst winters on record, as snow and ice brought the country to a halt and made pitches unplayable. Orient did not play after a 5-1 defeat at Leicester City on Boxing Day until their 3rd round FA Cup tie against Hull City, which had been postponed on numerous occasions since the beginning of January, was finally played on 11 February.

This decimation of the game, resulted in the creation of the Football Pools Panel in early 1963, overseen by five ex-players and officials for the major pools companies, including of course Littlewoods, led by John Moores the Everton chairman. Three people, former players, still meet from November to April every weekend to give their prediction of how any postponed match would have been played out.

Having won those four matches by the end of September, Leyton Orient would only win two more league matches all season, both in the months of April and May. They would beat Bolton Wanderers at Burnden Park 1-0 and Liverpool 2-1 at Brisbane Road where with relegation now a certainty less than 9,000 turned up.

Johnny had a notable meeting with the Leyton Orient board as relegation became a real probability, with Lew Grade asking him what it would cost to keep Orient up. Johnny replied, *'Keep your money, Mr Grade, you have had your fun. This is a dream.'* In time, just as the phrase *'Taxi for'* carries on in Everton folklore, the line *'Keep your money'* is still recalled by Brisbane Road supporters. Some wondering to this day what might have happened if Johnny had taken a different tone and tested the commitment of the wealthy board members. Could it have been the 60s equivalent of the Roman Abramovich effect that the Russian oligarch provided for Chelsea in the 2000's?

Poignantly, while Johnny Carey was devastated to have been relegated as Leyton Orient manager after gaining them promotion for their first, and still the only time to the English top flight, their last fixture would take him back to Old Trafford to face Manchester United. It could very well have been a must-win game for United, as they had more than skirted with relegation themselves since football had returned after the 'Big Freeze', and only a 1-1 draw at neighbours Manchester City had put City down and kept United up. While their league form had deteriorated, United had a great FA Cup run and the week after the fixture with Leyton Orient would be playing at Wembley against Leicester City in the final, which they won 3-1.

Old Trafford would turn out to be Johnny Carey's last match in charge of Leyton Orient, he was about to be attracted to the opportunity to lead Nottingham Forest…

As we did at the end of Johnny's travels at Blackburn Rovers and Everton, let his wife Margaret Carey have the last word on Leyton Orient. *'It was a long way from Lancashire to London for us when Jack got the Leyton Orient job, but it seemed a good idea at the time. Unfortunately, we had to leave our elder son Michael behind as he was then working for an advertising firm in Manchester and they had just offered him a promotion. We decided to let him stay with friends in Southport. By this time Gerald, our other son, had attended two primary schools and was about to attend his third grammar school. Life is hard for Football Manager's children. Leyton Orient was a lovely, homely club - probably still is and don't let anyone say in my presence that Londoners are cold and stuck up. I found them delightful people, with a lively sense of humour.*

Nevertheless, when Nottingham Forest offered Jack their management job, being a much larger club and let's admit it, a little nearer home, he accepted but not without a lot of heart searching. Jack loved that little club and particularly the chairman, Mr Harry Zussman. He hated having to tell them. Patricia was then three years old and making her third move. As we had left Michael behind in Southport, we left Gerald behind in Woodford Green. He was in his second year in the sixth form, and we felt it would be disastrous for him to leave at that time. So once again, we left a son with a friend.'

Chapter Twelve

SO NEARLY A DOUBLE

The approach from Nottingham Forest came to Johnny Carey after the 1962-63 season had finished, with newspapers reporting in early June that he had accepted a £3,000 a year contract with the East Midlands club. There had been speculation that Liverpool manager Bill Shankly had been at the top of the Forest wish list, which was at the time considered one of football's top, and safest, managerial positions. Billy Walker who had led Nottingham Forest to the 1959 FA Cup victory over Luton Town, had been in the post for over 20 years when he retired in 1960. He had been succeeded by Andy Beattie who Johnny replaced for the start of the 1963-64 season. Nottingham Forest also had a different set up off the field to most clubs as they were run by a committee as opposed to a board of directors.

When he arrived at the City Ground, Johnny found a very settled side. Nottingham Forest had finished ninth in the Football League in the previous season with a team that included: Peter Grummitt in goal; Peter Hindley and Denis Mochan at full-back; a half-back line of Jeff Whitefoot (who had played in Johnny's last league match for Manchester United at Middlesbrough in 1953); Bob McKinley, a Scot at centre-half who had played for Forest in their FA Cup victory in 1959 and been ever-present since; and Henry Newton who had come through the Forest youth set up at left-half. Besides Colin Addison at inside-right though, Johnny identified the forward line as needing improvements. He went back to his old club Everton to sign centre-forward Frank Wignall for £20,000, a man who had scored goals for him at Goodison Park.

Figure 33 New Forest Manager

Losing 1-0 at home to Aston Villa was not a great start to Johnny's new reign at Forest, but he soon had them on a winning run of five matches so that by mid-October when Manchester United arrived at the City Ground, it was a top-four battle for the two of them. An excellent match saw United win 2-1 but Forest had seemed to emphasise their credentials.

The good start was dissipated as Forest struggled for consistency. A 6-1 hammering at Everton after Christmas was not a result Johnny Carey would have relished, one of his former Blackburn Rovers youngsters Fred Pickering, scored a hat-trick for Everton on his debut in this match. Forest themselves had made a couple of significant signings, both forwards, with outside-left Alan Hinton joining from Wolverhampton Wanderers in January 1964 and John Barnwell from Arsenal in March 1964.

Twelve months on from managing Leyton Orient in their last match of the season away to Manchester United, Johnny Carey took Nottingham Forest back to his former home for the last match of his first season in charge at Forest. Sadly, for him, he faced the same result, a 3-1 defeat. This left Forest in 13th position which was a drop from their previous season's 9th position. There had been some significant additions to the forward-line though, and despite the results, the football Forest played had been very attractive.

Following the signings of the previous season, Johnny further strengthened by signed the experienced outside-right Chris Crowe from Wolverhampton Wanderers, and in a positional switch had Jeff Whitefoot and Henry Newton swap right and left-half positions. This now gave him, he felt, the team to move Forest forward. A characteristic of those days was how managers tried to keep the same eleven, except for injury and loss of form of course. He did have a couple of younger players ready to push for places such as Sammy Chapman a versatile defender and a young outside-left called Ian Storey-Moore, who would in time become a highly-prized footballer.

The form in the 1964-65 season was much stronger and consistent than Johnny's first season, so much so that when Manchester United arrived in mid-January the usual sell out for their visit was viewed by as many television cameras as possible, one of them the new BBC *'Match of The Day'* team which showed highlights later that Saturday evening. This match drew even more coverage than normal as United's Denis Law made his return from a six-match ban, and duly opened the scoring after three minutes. He would score another goal while Forest's outside-left Alan Hinton scored two himself to leave a fine match deadlocked at 2-2 leaving both sides in the top five. Manchester United with their forward line now boasting the *'holy trinity'* of Bobby Charlton, Denis Law and the young prodigy George Best would go onto be champions this season. While under Johnny's management, Nottingham Forest improved dramatically to finish in fifth spot, their highest First Division placing for over 60 years.

Forest followed this rise by going on a long and successful tour of America and Canada during the summer, bringing back happy memories for Johnny who had, of course, toured there twice in his Manchester United playing days.

They came back for the start of the 1965-66 season which would be a notable year in the football world. It was the centenary of the Nottingham Forest club, a season which saw the introduction of substitutes, with one now being allowed, and of course, the excitement at the end of the season of the 1966 World Cup Finals being played in England for the first and to date, only time. The season started in fine style for Forest with a 2-2 draw away at Newcastle United being followed by an emphatic hammering of the champions, Manchester United at the City Ground.

Despite torrential rain which kept the normal full house for United's visit down to 33,744 (still Forest's second highest home attendance of the season), those present witnessed one of the great Nottingham Forest displays. 3-0 up at half-time, they soon increased this to 4-0 - against the champions remember. A couple of late goals made the final score of 4-2 more respectable for United. The manner of the performance which built on the previous season's excellent form raised high hopes that Forest would challenge even more strongly this year. When they then beat West Bromwich Albion at the City Ground 3-2 and went to Old Trafford and came away with a 0-0 draw, Forest were top of the league after four matches.

Sadly, for Johnny, the run of form wasn't to continue. The following six games brought five defeats and a draw as the season dramatically unravelled. The team eventually finishing in a very uncomfortable 18th position. Johnny was left clinging to the sage words of his old boss Matt Busby who told him that it takes five years to get your team playing as you want them to.

The Nottingham Forest Chairman and their committee continued to back Johnny. They authorised the signings of Wales right-half Terry Hennessey from Birmingham City in November 1965 for over £50,000, and then in February 1966 the Scottish centre-forward Joe Baker from Arsenal for £65,000. So, Johnny could not be in any doubt that he needed to find consistent success for Nottingham Forest after two poor and one successful season in charge.

The committee's faith was rewarded, as in 1966-67, Nottingham Forest would have a very successful season. They finished runners-up in the Football League, their highest ever position at that point in their history, and, reached the semi-final of the FA Cup. Indeed, at times during the season, an incredible double was on the cards.

1966-67 SEASON

A feelgood factor for football followed on from the historic success of England and their famous World Cup victory, when they defeated West Germany 4-2 at Wembley Stadium in late July 1966. As the new season approached football was the main topic of conversation throughout the country

One very astute move Johnny made was to appoint Tommy Cavanagh as his coach. Tommy was not a shrinking violet, and after a playing career at Huddersfield Town and Doncaster Rovers, the Liverpool born footballer went into management, most recently at Brentford where Johnny had seen somebody who he thought would help him transform what was a decent team on paper into a proper team on the pitch. Tommy would go on to be coach at Manchester United under Tommy Docherty and later Dave Sexton, where he is remembered fondly by the fans. Tommy's daughter, Deborah, recalls her father's feelings for Johnny Carey: *'My dad admired and respected Johnny deeply. He always said he was a great man. They remained lifelong friends when their football paths parted. Johnny and his wife were dear friends of my Dad and Mam.'*

The side was still built around the consistent centre-half, Bob McKinley; with Peter Grummitt in goal, the full-backs were Peter Hindley and local youth player John Winfield; relative new signing Terry Hennessey at right-half and Henry Newton at left-half; Chris Crowe and Alan Hinton or Ian Storey-Moore on the wings; with Joe Baker and Frank Wignall expected to provide the goals aided by the prompting of inside-right John Barnwell. The team responded with good, consistent results, playing excellent flowing football. It certainly helped that Johnny was able to keep a virtually unchanged side until injuries came late in the season just as a possible 'double' was on the cards, but even so, he took Nottingham Forest to, what was their best all-round season ever at that time.

At the start of the 1966-67 season, four teams were considered the leading sides in English football. They were the current champions Liverpool, who had also been the champions in 1964 and FA Cup winners in 1965 (the team incidentally that had been promoted with Johnny Carey's 1961-62 Leyton Orient side). Next, Johnny's old playing club Manchester United who had won the FA Cup in 1963 and the league in 1965. Finally, a couple of London clubs, Tottenham Hotspur who did the double in 1960-61, slightly in decline but including the incomparable Jimmy Greaves in their side, and Greaves' old club Chelsea under the flamboyant managership of Tommy Docherty.

Johnny's Nottingham Forest were very far from that expected group of challengers for this season...

When Forest lost their opening two matches, both by 2-1, at home to Stoke City and away to Chelsea, it seemed to confirm that they were still a long way off from being in the running for either of English football's great trophies. Keeping the 2-1 scoreline going, this time in Forest's favour at Sheffield United, kick-started a decent run of six matches unbeaten, leading to the first real test of their credentials as Manchester United came into town on 1 October 1966.

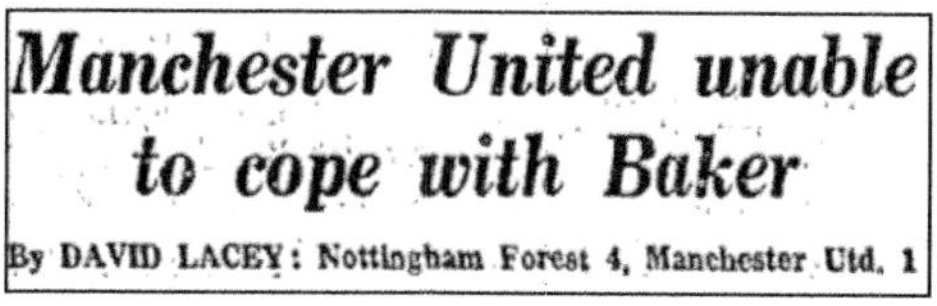

Manchester United unable to cope with Baker
By DAVID LACEY: Nottingham Forest 4, Manchester Utd. 1

Figure 34 'United unable to cope'

Forest were in ninth position, two points behind Manchester United in fifth position. The United side included recent World Cup winners Bobby Charlton and Nobby Stiles, the now fully established and brilliant George Best, and a new record signing for a goalkeeper in Alex Stepney, although they were without the injured Denis Law. Johnny had eight players who had played all nine previous matches that season and his team produced a fantastic free-flowing display that simply overwhelmed Manchester United as centre-forward Joe Baker ran Nobby Stiles ragged. Goals from Frank Wignall and a hat-trick, including a penalty, from winger Chris Crowe producing a stunning 4-1 victory for Forest.

An aside to the coverage of football 50 years or so ago, is that whilst Match of The Day on a Saturday night was literally that, one match of the day, other games would be covered on local ITV regions the following day. The Forest v United match being covered by an A.B.C. Television camera team who would transmit it on Midlands ITV in their Sunday *'World of Soccer'* feature. Indeed, this fixture always produced the largest crowd of the season, Manchester United being the visitors when the record was set in 1957, and it would be them who broke the record again in the 1967-68 season. This game on 1 October 1966 was watched by 41,854, a huge crowd when you consider that in any of the previous four home games the crowd had not exceeded 23,000!

Unfortunately, for Nottingham Forest, in what would eventually prove to be a decisive period of poor form, this victory over Manchester United would prove to be their only success in six matches which included a 4-0 defeat at champions Liverpool. By 12 November, and the home match against Sunderland, Forest were back down to ninth position which prompted Johnny to once again enter into the transfer market. He signed outside-right Barry Lyons from Rotherham United, replacing Chris Crowe, the man whose hat-trick against Manchester United seemed a lifetime away.

It did the trick! Forest beat Sunderland 3-1 and would go from 12 November until 11 February unbeaten, a run of 14 fixtures that included a double over Everton at Christmas, propelling them right into the mix. So much so, that by the time the 11 February fixture came around, away to Manchester United, Forest were third behind United and Liverpool with only two points separating the three of them.

Figure 35 Johnny with his pipe

Before the match, Johnny was seen calmly walking down the player's tunnel at Old Trafford, smoking his pipe and wearing a trilby, looking thoroughly in control back at his old stomping ground. As always, he received a wonderfully warm welcome from his former fans in the capacity crowd. Johnny reflected on the match beforehand. *'Some months ago, I decided that was needed was a harder approach, which Tommy Cavanagh has achieved, although I must emphasise we are not a tough side. Forest have always had a fine reputation as a footballing side, and I would not have it otherwise. I have always been a believer that pure football is a necessity, even in modern competitive conditions, but we have now added the necessary endeavour. Our players are fighting harder and helping one another.'*

Jack Crompton, a former colleague of Johnny Carey's, the goalkeeper in many of his greatest days as a Manchester United footballer, including the famous 1948 FA Cup Final victory over Blackpool, was now Manchester United's trainer. He added his thoughts on his former skipper in the match programme. *'He was the greatest skipper I have known in my career in the game, probably the finest there has ever been. He was undemonstrative, leading always by example, and everything he did, on or off the field, was for the benefit of the team by his own ability, and he carried out pre-match instructions to the letter, never trying to implant his own ideas into a particular match. He was marvellous with younger players, continually encouraging them with a kind word rather than a reprimand if anything went wrong.'*

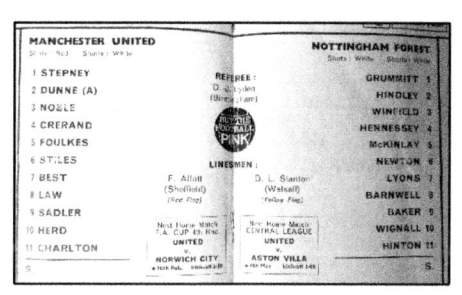

Figure 36 Line-ups, Manchester United v Nottingham Forest

The match befitted two top sides, strong defence from Forest against the exciting United attack, with the speedy Joe Baker always likely to score a vital goal on the break for the visitors. Peter Grummitt was an excellent goalkeeper, and in this match, he played one of his greatest games repeatedly thwarting the likes of Denis Law, Bobby Charlton, David Herd and George Best. The capacity crowd was settling for a goalless draw when with five minutes to go, Grummitt produced another fantastic save from Denis Law which went for a corner. Law was not finished, however, and from the corner, he produced an incredible overhead kick which beat even Grummitt. After the game, Matt Busby entered the Forest dressing room and invited Johnny and his entire team to the Manchester United boardroom, with both parties hoping one of them would be the eventual champions. Johnny had an insightful comment to make about a particular Manchester United player in this match, *'George Best was the finest footballer I ever saw. He had everything, the highest compliment I can make that not even Stanley Matthews or Tom Finney of my time, had all the qualities that George possessed.'*

United and Forest would not be meeting in the FA Cup, however, as United lost the week after to Second Division Norwich City in the 4th round, while Forest easily beat Newcastle United 3-0 following their 3rd round 2-1 victory over Plymouth Argyle. This brought Third Division Swindon Town to face Forest, and they produced battling displays holding out for 0-0 and 1-1 draws before in the third match, played at neutral Villa Park, home of Aston Villa, Forest finally showed their class and won 3-0. This earned them a home 6th round tie against the FA Cup holders Everton, a side that included two of England's World Cup heroes in Alan Ball and Ray Wilson.

To show that Forest were the real deal this season, after the heartbreak of losing to a late goal in the Old Trafford thriller, they went onto another long unbeaten run of 13 matches, making only one defeat in 27 fixtures from 12 November 1966 until 19 April 1967.

Included in that run was the epic sixth round FA Cup tie with Everton at the City Ground. That Forest would eventually win the match 3-2 and secure a semi-final place against Tottenham Hotspur at Hillsborough, was only part of the story. Ian Storey-Moore's displays and vital goals that season had seen him move into the left-wing position ahead of Alan Hinton and in this match, he would make himself a Nottingham Forest legend by scoring a hat-trick, as Forest came from 2-1 down to win the tie 3-2. Another Forest player who had made himself extremely popular with the Forest fans was centre-forward Joe Baker, big money signing from Arsenal the previous season. Quickly nicknamed 'Zigger Zagger', Joe had electric pace and was vital to Forest's style of play. Sadly, he was to receive a bad injury in the first half of the quarter-final which was to prove costly in the push for glory of the coming weeks. Alan Hinton came on to replace Joe Baker with Ian Storey-Moore going into the centre-forward position from where he caused Everton all sorts of problems as he proved the match winner. That final goal produced scenes of real danger as at one point a crush barrier collapsed producing a commentary by Kenneth Wolstenholme on 'Match of The Day' where he uttered the words *'the inevitable casualties of cup-ties'*. A further 22 years on at Hillsborough for the Liverpool v Nottingham Forest semi-final those words would sadly be truer than ever.

Joe Baker's injury caused him to miss important matches, including a rearranged league match at Sunderland and the semi-final versus Tottenham Hotspur. Both were lost, virtually ending the double dream that had been very much on. Sunderland won the league match on 19 April 1-0 at Roker Park and in the semi-final on 29 April, Tottenham Hotspur ended Forest's Wembley dream by winning 2-1. That was a bitter pill for Forest as they had dominated most of the game against a Tottenham side that was filled with star players. Spurs had Pat Jennings in goal, Alan Mullery and Dave MacKay at wing-half, Alan Gilzean and Jimmy Greaves provided a fearsome attack, and they even had the luxury of that excellent winger Cliff Jones on the subs bench if needed. It was their centre-half Mike England, a player Johnny Carey had nurtured in his time at Blackburn Rovers, who started the attack that ended in a Jimmy Greaves goal after half-an-hour that put Tottenham into the lead. Forest had much the better of that half-hour and then had much of the play after, but the absence of Joe Baker was proving to be a vital loss, not helped when Frank Wignall also took a knock. Frank Saul scored a second with 15 minutes left, and a Terry Hennessey's last-minute goal was scant consolation. It was Tottenham Hotspur who would contest the 1967 FA Cup Final against Chelsea.

Johnny Carey would finally lead Nottingham Forest to the runners-up position, four points behind champions Manchester United in the 1966-67 season. It was then the most successful overall season for the club, as Johnny recalled. *'We beat Manchester United who would win the league 4-1 and lost late on, away 1-0, possibly deserving a draw. Joe Baker had a fine season for us, and his injury in the quarter-final against Everton cost us dear. In many ways, it reminded me of the 1949-50 season as Manchester United captain when we finished runners-up to Portsmouth and lost, in a replay, to Wolverhampton Wanderers in the semi-final. I was so near to a double as a player and a manager.'*

1967 TO 1970 AT NOTTINGHAM FOREST

After their marvellous 1966-67 season, Nottingham Forest's then chairman Tony Wood had grand plans to make significant ground improvements at the City Ground. Tony Wood was very ambitious, perhaps too much so. Later this season he, rather than Johnny, would sanction a significant transfer for the Scottish international Jim Baxter, who had without doubt been a magnificent footballer, but sadly, by this stage of his career had too many problems to enable him to be consistently brilliant.

Before that though, Johnny, despite his extensive involvement in European football from his time as a player, as captain, then manager of the Republic of Ireland national side, experienced his first taste of European club action as Forest entered the Inter-Cities Fairs Cup, the forerunner of the present Europa League.

Forest were drawn against Eintracht Frankfurt in the first round with the first-leg away in Frankfurt. Eintracht, of course, were remembered for their part in that memorable European Cup Final of 1960 played in Glasgow against Real Madrid. A match, which although they lost 7-3 is still recalled as one of the great European Finals. The first-leg drew a sparse crowd of 4,500 but a Joe Baker goal gave Forest an excellent start to their European campaign. Home advantage was enforced in the second leg as Forest won 4-0 before over 27,000 delighted fans.

The next tie would be against FC Zurich, but before the first-leg home tie, Forest entertained Manchester United, the team that had stopped their championship dream of the previous season. United were also in Europe this season. Indeed they would go onto win their first ever European Cup by beating Benfica in an emotional Wembley final in May 1968. The league match at the City Ground in late October 1967 attracted the highest ever crowd at The City Ground, with 49,946 squeezing in. Both sides had made a steady start to the season, both having the extra games in Europe of course, but it was Forest who turned on the style as they deservedly won 3-1 to push themselves up the table.

With the extra confidence of beating the champions, it was a perfect time to play FC Zurich, but an away goal from the Swiss side in a 2-1 victory for Forest would eventually prove crucial. The second leg saw Zurich win 1-0 at home, sending Forest out on the away goal rule. This was where Chairman Tony Wood's ambitious were fully revealed to the travelling press as they flew back from Zurich. He felt that, as nearby Sheffield could host semi-finals so could Nottingham, and had planned extensions to the stadium before he had sanctioned the transfer of Jim Baxter from Sunderland. The problem was Baxter was going downhill form wise and was not what Johnny really wanted, with his team beginning to show their limitations after their heroics of the previous season.

Regardless, Jim Baxter was signed for £100,000 in December 1967, and it would not be a success, to say the least! Baxter, once the darling of Glasgow Rangers and all Scotland, had seen his form plummet. With personal problems also increasing, he was seen by many as a disruption in the dressing room. Only the previous April he had destroyed England at Wembley Stadium - England the holders of the World Cup being humiliated as Baxter led the Scots to a famous 3-2 victory. He did not look fit on his arrival in Nottingham though, and over the next 18 months would only play 49 matches and is still considered by many as among the worst signings in Nottingham Forest's history. It would also be one of the daggers in Johnny Carey over the next year. Johnny reflected that *'Transfer deals are one of the worst perils facing a football manager.'* Jim Baxter certainly would be as far as Johnny would be concerned.

Forest's form was patchy during the start of 1968. A fourth round FA Cup defeat at Leeds United and then a run of seven matches without a victory around Easter was compounded by a 6-1 hammering at Liverpool on the last day of the season. Johnny was not having the same effect on his side as he had in the previous season, and Forest would finish in 11th position. Johnny certainly knew that improvements would once again be required in the 1968-69 season…

In the fourth match of the 1968-69 season, Nottingham Forest were dealt a disastrous blow, which would mark a turning point in Johnny's fortunes. After a slow start of three draws and a defeat, Forest welcomed Leeds United to the City Ground. On 24 August 1968 a crowd of 31,126 were present for what seemed a tasty match on paper. The free-flowing Forest led by speedy centre-forward Joe Baker, hopefully, being prompted by midfielder Jim Baxter, against the Don Revie Leeds side built on a steely defence with a midfield of Billy Bremner and John Giles who were as good as any around. Just as half-time approached, with the score level at 1-1, the main stand suddenly and alarmingly took alight, with panic ensuing. Thankfully, nobody was killed, but the shock, surprise and fear were something those present would never want to repeat.

Stadium Safety

Like most sports, football was initially played in any open space, such as a park or on private land. As the popularity of the game, increased people began to turn up to watch the matches, standing on the sidelines and cheering on their team. As numbers grew, so too did the facilities for spectators. Soon areas, where the crowds could sit, were erected, allowing people to watch the games in comfort.

Standing sections were initially in the form of banks of earth, often later covered in railway sleepers or terraces. Initial structures were developed in a haphazard fashion, and in the first major disaster at UK football a terrace collapsed at Glasgow Rangers in 1902, resulting in the deaths of 25 people and serious injury to hundreds more. As a result, terraced sections that were not supported with solid earth were banned. Nevertheless, terraces remained rudimentary and, post-war crowds were huge. In 1946 a crush amongst the estimated 85,000 spectators at Bolton Wanderers resulted in the deaths of 33 people and countless more injuries.

It was a miracle that there were no casualties during the fire at Nottingham Forest on 24 August 1968 during the match with Leeds United. The Main Stand had been rebuilt in 1965, so the fire that broke out there, in a faulty boiler could not be blamed on ageing facilities. The fire rapidly tore through the stand's wooden construction entirely destroying it. Just three years later in 1971, again at Glasgow Rangers - 66 people died in a crowd crush near the end of a match with Celtic. The incident occurred when fans leaving the stadium were met by a group trying to return after hearing that Rangers had scored an equaliser.

1985 was a black year for English Football with two disasters involving English Football fans. In the Heysel disaster in Brussels, 39 mostly Juventus supporters died after crowd trouble with Liverpool fans resulted in a collapsing wall in an ageing stadium. Six hundred were injured that day. The fire at Bradford City on 11 May 1985 serves as a stark reminder of just how fortunate the fans present at the fire at Forest in 1968 were. Again, a fire tore rapidly through a wooden stand during a match. This time the results were tragic – with 56 dead and over 250 casualties.

Finally, the worst disaster in UK football history occurred at Hillsborough on 15 April 1989 where Liverpool were playing Nottingham Forest in the FA Cup semi-final. The 96 deaths at this match following from the events at Bradford and Heysel finally marked a turning point in football stadium safety. Terraces were banned, and safety regulations overhauled completely. Thankfully, to date, there have been no equivalent disasters in the UK since 1989

Figure 37 Johnny surveys the damage.

Those in front of the stand were quickly brought onto the pitch, with the players obviously also remaining as their dressing rooms were affected as the stand was severely damaged. Johnny Carey immediately searched for his wife Margaret who was present at the game, thankfully they were quickly reunited. What could have been a terrible disaster for human life, still had a terrible impact on Nottingham Forest Football Club. For Johnny, it must have been a particularly poignant memory of his seeing Old Trafford burning after the German bomber blitz 27 years earlier. On a lighter note, the Police chief in charge later said he never knew so many footballers had Rolex watches as per insurance claims!

The immediate task was to secure a venue for the forthcoming fixtures. The first of these would have been the usual sell out against Manchester United in early September, but that was cancelled until later in the season and home matches from the Football League cup tie with West Bromwich Albion, were played at Notts County's Meadow Lane ground just across the way. This would also entail six home league matches up until the visit of Liverpool at the end of November.

By then Forest had only achieved one victory all season, and the week before Liverpool's visit they had an away fixture at fellow strugglers Queens Park Rangers, both sides in the bottom three. A 2-1 defeat left even the normally mild-mannered Johnny full of anger as he kept his team in the dressing room venting his frustration at his team's performances. The fire was a definite factor, but a team including players such as big signings Joe

Baker, Jim Baxter, and Terry Hennessey, along with Forest legend Bob McKinlay should have been producing better performances.

While Liverpool did come to the City Ground and inflict another defeat by a single goal, the performance by Forest was much improved, and the side went onto their best run of three games unbeaten including a couple of victories. The end of the year though arrived with Nottingham Forest deep in relegation trouble, and as is often the case, the manager pays the ultimate price.

In a far more civilised way than Everton, Nottingham Forest and Johnny Carey parted company just as 1969 was on its way. The Forest chairman Tony Wood though expressed his personal sadness at the turn of events. *'Johnny Carey is one of nature's gentlemen. Personally, I don't think there is a nicer fellow in football. I feel he is one of the greatest administrators in the game, but we feel the need for a change.'*

Margaret Carey recalls her memories of a five-year time in the East Midlands. *'Jack and I had five very pleasant years in Nottingham. The year we moved from London in 1963, our eldest son Michael married Phyllis and was doing extremely well in his advertising world being a director of his own agency in Manchester. When Forest sacked Jack, I know wives are prejudiced when it comes to judging these things, but I have tried to look at it from all sides, and his removal still remains a mystery. In 1968 Nottingham Forest had a dreadful fire which burned down the main stand, dressing rooms etc. which meant they had to play their matches elsewhere. Notts County kindly leant them their stadium, but it was very upsetting to everyone concerned in a hundred niggly ways. It naturally had some bearing on the team's performances, but after all, it was only halfway through the season. Jack had a lot of success with Forest, but we left without bitterness as we had now learned that is the only way. A football manager's life must be one of the loneliest in the world. Jack was then offered several jobs in football but was feeling disenchanted with the game. For a few weeks, he was quite shattered. After all, it is a bit of a shock to go into work and come home a couple of hours later jobless. He had hundreds of letters from Nottingham people who were really hurt and ashamed that their club would do such a thing.'*

Johnny Carey was a football man through and through, and a return to one of his old clubs would offer him a further go at the game he loved. Before that though, since 1955 Johnny had also managed his much-loved country, the Republic of Ireland alongside his various club duties until 1967. Let us now look at the 'other' life of Johnny Carey, football manager.

Chapter Thirteen

AN BANISTEOIR

Alongside his club management career, Johnny Carey was manager, or 'banisteoir' in Gaelic, of the Republic of Ireland team. Actually, neither the English nor the Gaelic word captures the reality of what Johnny Carey became in 1955 when he was asked to take charge of his national side. Although Johnny would manage the team on the day, Ireland, like a lot of nations then, still had a committee who selected the players for internationals. His task was to make a winning team out of the names he was given on match day. The main Irish league sides of the 1950's were: St Patrick's Athletic; Shamrock Rovers; Drumcondra and Dundalk. The Ireland committee members would invariably come from Dublin, Cork, Galway and Limerick, but the majority of international class players would have crossed the Irish Sea and be playing in England. England also operated this way at the time, with Walter Winterbottom the England, team manager. Winterbottom had been a teammate of Johnny's on his debut for Manchester United back in 1937.

When appointed in 1955, Johnny Carey was in his third season as the Blackburn Rovers manager and this dual role of leading Ireland and whichever club side he was currently managing lasted until February 1967. By then Johnny had led Everton, Leyton Orient and Nottingham Forest besides Blackburn Rovers.

Back in 1954 FIFA had decreed that the Football Association of Ireland (FAI) would now be called the Republic of Ireland for international fixtures and Johnny Carey was determined to improve the fortunes of the nation where he was born. There was an early incident as Ireland offered a £20 match fee plus expenses for Johnny. When Johnny asked his friend, Peter Doherty one of Northern Ireland's most celebrated footballers and then their team Manager, what the North was paying, Johnny was told £50 plus expenses! It was not the money Johnny was interested in though, he already had his salary from Blackburn Rovers, and he was quoted as saying, *'I want to make a success of the job as opposed to the money element'*. Still, though, it did perhaps show a comparatively amateur approach from the Ireland committee.

Of the 45 international matches that Johnny would lead Ireland, 23 would be World Cup and European Nations Cup (which then became the European Championships) fixtures. England and Scotland would feature in World Cup qualifiers as Ireland's opponents, as would Czechoslovakia who went on to be World Cup runners-up in 1962, while in the European Nations Cup competition, Spain winners of the 1964 tournament had to overcome a play-off in the quarter-finals to beat Ireland. The 22 friendly games would include fixtures against the World Cup holders from 1954 West Germany, and the

1958 World Cup finalists Sweden. Overall Johnny would win 17, draw 7 and lose 21. He had an excellent start. Of his first seven internationals, Ireland would win 4, draw 2 and lose just 1. Four of these matches were qualifying games for the 1958 World Cup due to be staged in Sweden.

> ### *International Football in Ireland*
> *The story of football, and international football in particular, on the island of Ireland is a complicated one. When Johnny was born in Dublin in 1919 Ireland was part of the United Kingdom, and the Union Flag flew over public buildings. Sport in Ireland though was strongly influenced by the Gaelic Athletic Association (GAA) which had been formed in 1884 to preserve Ireland's traditional sports – the most popular being Gaelic Football and Hurling. Football was viewed as a non-Irish sport by the GAA and indeed watching or playing association football was considered a disciplinary offence by the GAA until 1971.*
>
> *It is no surprise then, that at least initially, association football was most popular amongst the Protestant population in the Northern Counties of Ireland. The development and governance of the game in Ireland was of necessity intertwined with the political events that led to the partition of Ireland into Northern and Southern Ireland in 1921 and the founding of the Irish Free State in 1922.*
>
> *Initially, association football throughout Ireland was governed by the Irish Football Association (IFA) which was formed in 1880. The IFA was dominated by Northern clubs from the Belfast Area. It is the fourth oldest national football association in the world (after only England, Scotland and Wales) and is still the governing body of football in Northern Ireland. In 1882 Ireland played their first international against England, losing 13-0 a record score for England and (Northern) Ireland to this day. Shortly after partition in 1921, a dispute over the venue for a replay between Glentoran (Belfast) and Shelbourne (Dublin) led to the formation of the rival Football Association of Ireland which was established to govern the game in what became the Irish Free State. This led to the situation where both bodies, the Belfast based IFA and the Dublin based FAI claimed to represent football throughout the whole of the island. Each association competed internationally under the name 'Ireland' and selected players from both the rival national leagues, which had also split. The world governing body FIFA ruled that the FAI were the official organisers of the 26 counties of the republic, whereas the IFA had the same status in Northern Ireland.*
>
> *Nevertheless, the IFA national team continued to select players from the whole of Ireland until 1950. This gave rise to some very unusual situations and conflicts of interest. One notable example being when Johnny played for both 'Irelands' in the space of three days, both times against England. In the first match on 28 September 1946 Carey represented 'Ireland' in Belfast losing 7-2 and two days later on 30 September 30 represented (the Republic of) 'Ireland' in a 1-0 defeat to the same England side. In 1954, four years after renouncing their claim to represent the whole of Ireland the IFA officially adopted the name "Northern Ireland".*

It was Sunday 27 November 1955 when Johnny's international life part two, started with the visit of Spain to Dalymount Park, Dublin. As with the majority of his players, Johnny would have had to dash to Dublin from his league fixture. In his case leaving a league match at home to Swansea Town, which Blackburn had won 3-0, to go to Liverpool and catch the B&I ferry overnight to Ireland. On arrival at around 7am, he then went to the Gresham Hotel to meet 'his' team at 12 o'clock on Sunday, just hours before the 2:30 pm kick-off time. Actually, ten of the starting eleven were based in England, with only centre-forward Gibbons, from the St Patrick's Athletic club, being based in Ireland. Perhaps surprisingly, the Republic of Ireland played the majority of their home fixtures on a Sunday, which was still a very religious day in the country. The Catholic Church, however, took the view that as long as people went to Mass beforehand, then there was nothing wrong with watching, or playing, in the afternoon. The first Republic of Ireland team that Johnny would be asked to motivate coach and lead was: O'Neill; Dunne; Cantwell; Farrell; Martin; Ryan; Ringstead; Fitzsimons; Gibbons; Cummins and Eglington.

A goal from Arthur Fitzsimons in the first ten minutes was a great start which the 35,000 crowd warmly appreciated. Spain were a very decent side though, containing players from Real Madrid, who would become the first ever European Cup winners the following June, and the team who would be Spanish champions that season, Atletico Bilbao. They would regroup and go 2-1 up by half-time. This then, was where Johnny would get one of his few opportunities to calmly convey his thoughts to his new side, having barely had time to practice or even really spending much time on their roles. After his deliberations, where the words *'fizz it about'* would have been sure to have been uttered, he went back out, smoking his pipe hoping that his team talk would somehow have stimulated ideas and confidence in his players. They did, as Ireland fought tremendously in the second-half against top class opposition with Alf Ringstead scoring a deserved equaliser.

In future home matches, Johnny would use the couple of hours before kick-off at the Gresham Hotel to remind his players of his philosophy. He would want them to play accurate, quick football, keeping the ball on the ground. The quickness part demanded players move into open spaces, reminding them of the old football saying, *'that the ball travels quicker than the man'*.

One of his Blackburn Rovers players, Mick McGrath, recalled later that when Johnny managed both Blackburn Rovers and Ireland, there would be no mention of Ireland while they were at Ewood Park, but a couple of weeks before the international match they would receive details of all the arrangements from the FAI. There must have been worrying thoughts at Blackburn though, as, after this opening match for Johnny as a dual manager,

Rovers did not win for the next six games!

It would be out of season when Johnny was next asked to manage his country, an away friendly in Rotterdam against Holland in May 1956. Holland were not yet the free-flowing football nation they became in the 1970's, but any nation playing at home provided a difficult match for the opposition. A partisan crowd exceeding 60,000 for what was a friendly, saw a tight, closely fought, but goalless first half.

Johnny Carey had some new players involved in this match and one, Liam (Billy) Whelan was a player Johnny knew very well, as he was the first man to welcome Billy when he came over from Ireland to join Manchester United in 1953. This was at the time that Johnny was about to leave Old Trafford after his glorious footballing career, and Billy was about to join for what would also be a memorable, if so sadly, a shorter time. This match against Holland was Billy's first international and in the second-half he showed that he was entirely at ease in the company of fellow internationals, having, of course, helped Manchester United's team of young all-star players the 'Busby Babes' to win the First Division Championship recently.

Figure 38 Liam 'Billy' Whelan.

Billy's scheming and the half-time talk Johnny Carey had given to his side, saw a complete transformation in the second-half, as two goals from Arthur Fitzsimons and one apiece from Alf Ringstead and another new player for Johnny, Arsenal's left-winger Joe Haverty, saw Ireland 4-0 up with 20 minutes left. Despite a late consolation for Holland this was a wonderful victory for Ireland and set them up nicely for the World Cup fixtures with Denmark and England which would follow in the next 12 months.

The lack of competitive matches compounded by the lack of preparation time when the games came along was not an ideal situation for Johnny, though he dealt with it in his usual unflappable manner. Ireland, for example, would only play three internationals in each of the years 1956, 1957, 1958 and 1959. It would be early October 1956 when Johnny was next back managing Ireland, this time for a World Cup qualifier with Denmark in Dublin.

The qualifier was for the 1958 World Cup Finals due to be staged in Sweden, and Ireland were in a three-team group along with Denmark and England. The team at the top of the mini-league points wise would qualify, goal difference did not count, so if two sides finished equal on points there would have to be a play-off to determine the qualifier.

Because of the selection policy imposed upon him, Johnny would find players selected for him, that had not appeared in previous matches. The Denmark World Cup tie in October 1956 was a case in point, as the two Ireland goal scorers in a fine 2-1 victory were Dermot Curtis the Bristol City centre-forward and George Gavin the Norwich City winger. Whatever the selection issues, this time Ireland had a flying start as they sought World Cup qualification. The deciding matches would be against England, home and away, to be played in May 1957.

Before those matches, Ireland played a memorable friendly in November 1956, a month after their Denmark victory. The visitors were West Germany, at the time the World Cup holders after their stunning win in the 1954 final against the seemingly all-conquering Hungary. One blow for Johnny was Manchester United's request to have Billy Whelan left out as it was a friendly and he was involved in a top of the table league match in London at Tottenham Hotspur the day before. Billy was also playing a lot of games at the time, United had just completed a two-legged European Cup tie against, strangely enough, a German side, Dortmund Borussia who United had overcome 3-2 on aggregate.

In a famous victory for the Irish, they defeated the World Cup holders 3-0 before an ecstatic Dublin crowd. All three goals were scored in the second half, a Cantwell penalty, plus goals very late on from Haverty and McCann. It is perhaps a reflection on the wise tactical words of Johnny Carey at half-time that Ireland seemed to show improvement in a lot of second halves. Johnny would have to wait another six months to test his skill at international level again, but three victories and a draw in his first four internationals had Irish football fans looking forward to the double-header World Cup ties with England due in May 1957.

In those first four internationals that he had managed, Johnny's team had let just four goals in. By half-time in the match against England at Wembley Stadium, they were 4-0 down! The game was played on the Wednesday after the 1957 FA Cup Final in which Aston Villa had controversially beaten Manchester United. There would be five players who featured in that final appearing in the England v Republic of Ireland international, Roger Byrne, Duncan Edwards and Tommy Taylor for England, and Billy Whelan and Pat Saward for Ireland. The first four from Manchester United and Pat Saward from Aston Villa.

It certainly did not seem to affect Tommy Taylor that he was back at the scene of a disappointing loss, as he scored three first-half goals with John Atyeo from Bristol City getting the other England goal. Noel Cantwell, the Irish and West Ham United left-back, was undoubtedly wondering what Johnny's attitude would be as the team trooped back to the dressing room with such a large deficit as he recalled. *'I hardly dared to go into the dressing room as we were all playing badly and some of the lads were having a terrible time, I thought*

Johnny might blow his top, but he just stood at the door, smiling as we trooped in and said "Now then, let us see what we can do about this".'

Noel then explained how calmly Johnny spoke to the players, never once losing his head, telling them all what he thought had gone wrong, having words with those who were particularly overawed, simply encouraging them to do more. The Irish team did pull a goal back from Dermot Curtis and, indeed, Billy Whelan hit a shot against the bar at 4-1, but John Atyeo scored a fifth goal (his second), to leave England just needing to avoid defeat in Dublin in the second leg, to qualify for the 1958 World Cup Finals.

Billy Whelan was often seen as a quiet mild-mannered Irish lad, but Noel Cantwell recalled another side, Billy's impish sense of humour *'I recall an evening before the England match at Wembley when we were staying in our Weybridge hotel. While the entire team hung around the telephone in one room, convulsed in laughter, Billy rang our trainer in his room a few yards down the corridor, pretending to be a reporter from a well-known national newspaper asking for an interview. The trainer, Shamrock Rovers Billy Lord, agreed and while we listened in raptures, Billy Whelan's drawling voice wormed the entire life story out of Bill Lord, not sparing a detail. We never let on, and Bill Lord was still wondering days after what became of his article, and fee!'*

The second-half display at Wembley Stadium must have provided confidence for the return, which followed a mere 11 days later at Dalymount Park. That ground was only a mile from Billy Whelan's family home in Dublin, and he was desperate to put on a show. Inside three minutes he sent the packed 45,000 crowd wild as he beat two England players, one of whom was his club mate Duncan Edwards, before crossing to Alf Ringstead to head home. Billy nutmegged Duncan Edwards twice, which the brilliant England young star was not impressed with! This sort of confidence from Billy Whelan spread to his teammates, and they played quite magnificently as they dominated not just the first-half, but the whole match. Sadly, for the men in green, with the clock ticking towards 90 minutes, that superb footballer, Tom Finney, beat a couple of Irish defenders to cross for John Atyeo to score yet another goal in this two-legged tie and equalise. Despite the disappointment, Johnny had some consolation, seeing the real impact his Blackburn Rovers wing-half Ronnie Clayton had made in both these matches for England.

Eire were just foiled in thrill-a-minute World Cup-tie
ENGLAND SCRAPED INTO FINALS—BY 50 secs.

Figure 39 'Eire were just foiled'

Noel Cantwell remarked after the game the difference in eleven days from the hammering at Wembley Stadium to the happiness of the performance at Dalymount Park, could hardly be seen in Johnny's demeanour. Noel said, *'Johnny was exactly the same man whatever the result, at moments of triumph and despair he remained unruffled and level-headed. He was a great team manager in my opinion.'* Noel Cantwell was a man of Cork and another from there, Charlie Hurley, made his international debut in this match. Charlie was then a Millwall player and would go on to give superb service to the Irish team.

The last-minute draw would be enough for England to qualify for the 1958 World Cup finals in Sweden, but while they could not qualify, Ireland did have one more World Cup tie to fulfil, an away fixture in October 1957 against Denmark in Copenhagen. The game was played on 2 October. Incredibly this was the same night as the second leg European Cup tie between Manchester United and Shamrock Rovers, the Republic of Ireland champions, which precluded players from both sides for selection! Liam (Billy) Whelan would have been one of those players, although as it happened, he missed the European Cup tie at Old Trafford due to a flu epidemic of the time. Billy had set Dublin alight the week before as he scored twice leading Manchester United to an emphatic 6-0 victory, although Shamrock Rovers showed their abilities as they ran United to 3-2 in the second leg - a 9-2 aggregate victory.

Over in Copenhagen, Ireland produced a splendid display to do the double over the Danes by winning 2-0, the last-minute goal in the home draw with England proving the difference in the group. The Danish supporters though, were in uproar as the game plan Johnny devised was centred around a very well executed offside trap which continually frustrated the Danish forwards. Johnny was now getting a more settled side, but was to be dealt a devastating blow, both from an Ireland perspective and from his loyalties to Manchester United on 6 February 1958 when the Manchester United team, returning from an away European Cup tie in Belgrade, crashed on take-off from Munich airport after a stop to refuel. Eight players from the side known as the 'Busby Babes' were killed, one of them being young Dubliner Liam (Billy) Whelan.

Billy had only played four internationals for the Republic of Ireland but was most definitely one of the players Johnny would have hung his famous trilby on when planning the future for Ireland. The next fixture for them was a friendly in Vienna against Austria in March 1958, a mere month after the Munich air disaster and the thoughts of the team and management were obviously elsewhere as Austria comfortably won the match 3-1.

Ireland would have two more friendlies in 1958, both against Poland. The first in Katowice in May 1958 with over 80,000 watching, Ireland being the first team from the West to play in Poland since before the Second World War. The second match being in Dublin in October 1958. There was a near-perfect symmetry between the two games, both ending 2-2, with Noel Cantwell scoring both Ireland's goals in each match, one of them in both games being from the penalty spot. There was a significant difference as far as Johnny was concerned though, in the May match he had just led Blackburn

Rovers to promotion from the Second Division as well as reaching the FA Cup Semi-Finals, but when the teams met in October 1958 he was the new manager of Everton…

UEFA had created a new competition for international matches in the late 1950's called the European Nations Cup, which by 1968 became known as the European Championship as we still know it. The first final was to be played in 1960 with group matches played to qualify. The Republic of Ireland would host the first-ever tie in the competition in April 1959 against Czechoslovakia.

A crowd of over 42,000 packed into Dalymount Park to see this historic international and were ecstatic when local man Liam Tuohy of Shamrock Rovers scored what was the first ever goal in this famous competition. When the Irish captain, Noel Cantwell scored yet another penalty for his country, his third in successive matches, it was to give the Irish a winning 2-0 lead. So, Johnny became the first manager to win a European Nations international, another notch in his career. The second leg played a month later in Bratislava, saw the Czech's take an early lead to cut the deficit, which in the second-half was completely wiped out in a ten minute spell as Czechoslovakia finished 4-0 victors, winning 4-2 on aggregate, resulting in an early exit for Ireland. There was no shame in defeat though - Czechoslovakia were building a good side at the time, taking the third place in the final stages of this first ever competition in 1960 and would be serious challengers in the 1962 World Cup as the Irish were to find out to their cost in the qualifying group.

Johnny had real help in his years as the Republic of Ireland manager from senior professionals in the side. Players such as Noel Cantwell then of West Ham United later, like Carey a Manchester United FA Cup-winning captain, and that colossus of a centre-half Charlie Hurley of Millwall and Sunderland fame, gave the team a real gee-up when required.

The inspiration provided by Johnny was seen at first hand by a 19-year-old Dublin lad called Johnny Giles then playing for Manchester United and given his international debut against Sweden in Dublin in November 1959. The opposition had been runners-up in the 1958 World Cup, losing the final 5-2 in their own country to a Pele inspired Brazil. Giles recalled the impact of sharing a dressing room with these Irish football giants. *'Johnny Carey, the manager, gave us the team talk. This in itself was an awe-inspiring moment for me because Carey was an idol to me and all other Irish football following youngsters. Captain of the Manchester United team that had won the FA Cup in 1948, the Football League title in 1952, captained Rest of Europe against Great Britain in 1947, Footballer of the Year in 1949. Johnny Carey was "the man". He had this instruction to "fizz it about" probably one of the few things he had time to tell players who met up on the morning of the match in those days. His aura was enough for me, and probably all the other players in the side those days. In fact, it took me all my time to stop calling him Mister! Noel Cantwell was another who inspired, coming round to encourage, "settle down-enjoy it-get on the ball".'*

Incredibly, Ireland after going two goals behind to Sweden responded brilliantly with Johnny Giles scoring a spectacular debut international goal and then helping complete the turnaround in a famous 3-2 Irish victory. This was even more impressive when you consider Sweden had just beaten England 3-2 at Wembley Stadium. Johnny was quick to give his views on the potential of Johnny Giles, saying *'He is a wonderful player. He has a good football brain, and we are giving him the opportunity to use it, as are Manchester United'*.

So good was this victory that the FAI put a request in to be included in the British Home Championships. Johnny Carey commented, *'This is a great day for us beating a very fine Sweden side. We hope it is the beginning of a new era in Eire's football history.'*

Having played three internationals per year since Johnny took the managerial reins for Ireland in 1955, the pace increased, and in 1960 the Republic played five matches. One match was against the only South American country that Johnny faced in his 12-year international managerial career, when Chile visited Dublin in March 1960 as preparation for themselves hosting the 1962 World Cup Finals.

Continuing their fine form, Ireland beat Chile 2-0 in what was a very bad-tempered match, giving people an early insight as to what would later be seen in the 1962 World Cup held in Chile. This set Ireland up for a 'mini' European tour of matches against West Germany and then a return against Sweden. A tremendous 1-0 victory in Dusseldorf against West Germany before a crowd of 51,000 showed how far Ireland had progressed. So much so that Charlie Hurley regarded the victory as akin to Torquay United going to Old Trafford and winning! Johnny Carey's side was soon brought back to earth though when an excellent Sweden team gained revenge for their defeat in Dublin the previous November by winning 4-1.

At the end of September 1960, Johnny had an emotional managerial experience when his Ireland side met Wales for the very first time in Dublin. The opposition were managed by his former Manchester United assistant manager, the legendary Jimmy Murphy. Jimmy was still Matt Busby's right-hand man, the person who had almost single-handed, kept the club alive in the days after the Munich Air Disaster. A man that later in 1958 took Wales to an incredible quarter-final position in the World Cup in Sweden, only losing 1-0 to a Pele goal for Brazil, the eventual winners of that competition. Wales had also been without their talisman in that match, the quite superb John Charles, as they were again when they visited Dublin in 1960.

Included in their side though were a lot of seasoned internationals such as the Tottenham Hotspur wingers Terry Medwin and the outstanding Cliff Jones. At inside forward they had Phil Woosnam who in later years would make another name for himself as a top football administrator in America. Their other inside-forward was well known to Johnny, somebody who had been an integral part of Blackburn Rovers and who he had since signed for

Everton, Roy Vernon. It would be Jimmy Murphy though who had the upper hand against Johnny in this match as Wales won the friendly 3-2.

Ireland did end 1960 on a high though, as they beat Norway in Dublin 3-1 in early November. It was also the end of a quite incredible goal-scoring sequence for outside-right Fionan Fagan, predictably nicknamed Paddy by the various English sides he had played for, Hull City, Derby County, and most famously, Manchester City. While there, Paddy had been a vital part of the so-called 'Revie Plan' helping City reach two consecutive FA Cup Finals against Newcastle United and Birmingham City. Paddy Fagan would have the distinction of scoring the winner against West Germany, the consolation goal in Stockholm against Sweden, the two goals against Wales and the opening goal against Norway in Dublin.

By the time the Republic of Ireland played again, Johnny would no longer be the Everton manager. His undignified removal from Everton in the back of a taxi by chairman John Moores was a sensational story at the time.

Figure 40 Match Programme, Ireland v Scotland

While it left Johnny in limbo club wise, he was still very busy with the Ireland side as they had two internationals against Scotland in the 1962 World Cup qualifying group to be played over four days. The first at Hampden Park, the second at Dalymount Park. The sacking gave Johnny quality time with his side, firstly as they stayed at the Marine Hotel in Troon, a beautiful golf hotel as well which was much appreciated by keen golfer Johnny! While there, Johnny had a surprise visitor, the chairman of Greenock Morton who was very interested in taking him there as their manager. Johnny recalled the time, *'There was, thankfully, quite a bit of interest in taking me on as manager, indeed from one end of Britain in Plymouth Argyle to the visit from Greenock Morton. It was a very generous offer from them, but the move I settled on was to the then Second Division Leyton Orient.'*

As with the recent match against Wales, the game at Hampden Park would be the first international between the Republic of Ireland and Scotland. It was also the first match in the World Cup group that also included Czechoslovakia. The game at Hampden Park drew a crowd of 46,000, and the locals would go home very happy as their side won easily 4-1. Scotland had a strong team, with players such as Jim Baxter and Eric Caldow from Glasgow Rangers, Billy McNeill and Pat Crerand from Glasgow Celtic and Arsenal's David Herd in their line up and although Ireland came back into the game at 2-1, the Scots ran out comfortable winners.

Four days later an equally large crowd, this time 45,000 packed into Dalymount Park hoping for revenge, but two goals from Everton centre-forward Alex Young gave Scotland complete control as they won 3-0. Alex Young was one of three players who Johnny Carey had managed in his times at Everton and Blackburn Rovers playing in this match, Andy McEvoy of Rovers and Mick Meagan of Everton the others. Ireland's display though was heavily criticised in the press with the Irish Times claiming, *'it was one of the worst displays ever seen by an Irish team.'*

Ireland's next fixtures in October 1961, provided another two-legged tie in a World Cup qualifying group, this time against Czechoslovakia. Johnny would by then be in charge of Leyton Orient. If the Irish press felt the Scotland defeat was bad, they had more reason to criticise the performance in the Czechoslovakia matches, particularly the away fixture in Prague. The Czech side was a strong team as Ireland had seen a couple of years earlier in the European Nations matches, but two years on they were high class as Scotland had found out a week after their crushing victory over Ireland in Dublin when they were hammered 4-0 in Prague.

Johnny had a small band of players to choose from though, and Czechoslovakia came to Dublin in early October 1961 and won 3-1, although Johnny Giles had equalised in the first half with another top quality international goal. Two second-half strikes gave the Czech team a comfortable victory. If these last three matches had been hard for the Irish public to endure a real disaster was about to hit them. The return tie played in Prague at the end of October brought a then record defeat for the Irish side, as Czechoslovakia won 7-1. They were 4-0 up at half-time, and the hammering ended an inglorious attempt at qualification for the 1962 World Cup, in marked contrast to the glorious failure to qualify four years earlier. The result also cast light on the still amateur nature of international team management at the time. While Johnny Carey could not take any consolation from the match in Prague, he was not present, as his Leyton Orient side had a game against Leeds United at Elland Road to fulfil. Johnny had always made it clear that his first duty would be to whichever club he was employed by and the system worked comparatively well over his 12 years as national manager, with Johnny Carey only missing four Irish internationals. Czechoslovakia, on the other hand, proved their worth and having edged Scotland out as group winners via a play-off they went to Chile and reached the final of the World Cup, losing to the holders Brazil 3-1.

Sadly, the success Johnny was tasting in England in taking Leyton Orient to promotion was not replicated in Ireland. When Austria won 3-2 in Dublin in April 1962, his Ireland side were on a bad run of five successive defeats and six defeats in their last seven matches. Johnny must have felt at a real crossroads, but he was a fighter who was immensely proud Irishman and was determined to turn things around. This he certainly did, as Ireland would be undefeated in their next five internationals including fixtures in the European Nations Cup qualifiers for the 1964 finals.

The 1964 format meant two-legged ties would determine the winners until the semi-final stage with Ireland drawing Iceland in the preliminary round. These matches were played in August and September 1962 with the home match in Dublin first. After their poor run of performances, the Irish crowd hardly flocked in numbers to Dalymount Park for this match, although in fairness Iceland were hardly one of the big attractions in international football. A crowd of 20,000 did see a much better performance though, in a 4-2 home victory giving Ireland every hope of qualifying. The away match in Reykjavik saw a Liam Tuohy goal give Ireland a 1-1 draw and a first-round tie against Austria. This would be the second of the four games Johnny could not attend as Leyton Orient were involved in an East London 'derby' against West Ham United at Brisbane Road, a game they won 2-0.

As the next qualifying matches, against Austria, would not be played until a year later in September and October 1963, Johnny arranged a friendly against Scotland in Dublin in June 1963 a full eight months since Ireland had played a match. Johnny Carey himself was also the centre of football talk as he was about to leave Leyton Orient and become the Nottingham Forest manager.

It was only two years since Scotland had been in Dublin giving the Irish a football lesson, but on 9 June 1963, the Republic of Ireland and manager Johnny Carey got their football pride back as they secured a famous 1-0 victory. An early goal from Noel Cantwell playing as centre-forward, a month after he had emulated Johnny Carey's feat and led Manchester United to FA Cup Final glory by beating Leicester City 3-1 in the final, was then protected by a brilliant defensive performance from the Irish with centre-half Charlie Hurley outstanding.

Johnny was now able to call on more experience in his side. Although still selected by a committee based in the Republic, the team had become more settled. Alan Kelly of Preston North End was now a reliable goalkeeper, full-back Tony Dunne a regular at Manchester United as was Johnny Giles, Andy McEvoy, Mick McGrath and Joe Haverty were regulars at Blackburn Rovers, and these along with the well-established internationals Cantwell and Hurley formed the backbone of the side. Even so, this was a tremendous victory as Scotland had such as Denis Law, Jim Baxter, Billy McNeill, Willie Henderson and Frank McLintock amongst their side.

A 0-0 draw in Vienna against Austria followed, giving Johnny's Ireland side a real chance to reach the quarter-finals of the European Nations Cup. The result was especially creditable as Noel Cantwell, and Tony Dunne could not play as Manchester United were involved in their first European match after the Munich Air Disaster, playing Dutch side Willem 11. For the second leg, the Irish public turned up in numbers at Dalymount Park to support their green-shirted heroes, although they were quietened somewhat on 38 minutes when Austria went 1-0 up. Noel Cantwell restored parity as playing centre-forward again, he equalised before half-time bringing fans onto the pitch in celebration. An own goal by Austria, midway through the second-half sent them into a real frenzy before the Austrians equalised late on making a play-off looking probable. That was until a handball gifted Ireland a penalty in the last minute. Noel Cantwell duly converted, to put Johnny's team into the quarter-finals of a major football competition.

The quarter-final would be a tough two-legged tie against Spain, played in March and April 1964. A busy year during which, instead of the average three games, the Republic of Ireland would feature in six internationals. The first leg was to be played in the passionate Spanish city of Seville, with Johnny's task as manager being made even more difficult by circumstances elsewhere. Manchester United and Sunderland were involved in one of the FA Cup's greatest ties, which went to a second replay a couple of nights before the Spain match. United would not release Noel Cantwell and Tony Dunne as they felt whatever the result of the cup tie, they were involved in too many matches. Charlie Hurley was appearing for Sunderland in this trio of games, and by the time that he appeared in Seville, he would be playing his third match in five days on top of all the travelling involved.

Spain were a splendid side, players from Real Madrid and Barcelona joining together, with Madrid's Amancio having a superb match, helping Spain to completely overwhelm the Ireland side, being 4-1 up at half-time. Another inspiring talk by Johnny at least kept the score down to just one more goal, but the manner of the 5-1 victory left little doubt that, barring a miracle, the tie was over. Despite the Irish crowd in the home leg being as equally passionate as the Spaniards had been, Ireland were on the backfoot and battled hard to keep the score down to 2-0 and a 7-1 aggregate defeat. One consolation for Johnny and his team was that Spain went on to win the European Nations Cup, with the finals being played in their country. They beat the Soviet Union 2-1 in the final which no doubt brought great satisfaction to the country's leader, General Franco. He had ordered Spain not to play the Soviet Union in the 1960 finals as they had supported the Spanish Republicans against Franco in the Spanish Civil War.

Although one competition had gone, the next wasn't far away, and the opportunity of appearing in England for the 1966 World Cup Finals was next on the horizon for Johnny and his Ireland side. A further four friendlies would be played in 1964, home and away against Poland, a match in Oslo against Norway and a return to Dublin for England, seven years since the drama of their World Cup meeting there in 1957.

The Poland matches resulted in home wins for both nations, 3-1 to Poland in Warsaw and 3-2 to the Republic of Ireland in Dublin. Norway were comprehensively beaten 4-1 in Oslo, where Charlie Hurley scored two goals as a makeshift centre-forward, equalling Johnny's highest winning margin as the team manager, while the England game brought the usual strong emotions when the two countries opposed each other. Played in late May 1964, a packed Dalymount Park saw an England side being assembled by manager Alf Ramsey for the World Cup in two years' time. Just four members of what would be their World Cup-winning side, George Cohen, Ray Wilson, Bobby Moore and Bobby Charlton played in this match, which England won 3-1 with Jimmy Greaves, another player who would feature in the 1966 competition, scoring one of the England goals. This was the fifth occasion that England and the Republic of Ireland had played against each other, and Johnny had featured in all of them, twice as captain and three times as the manager, emphasising his unique position in the history of football in Ireland.

As 1965 arrived, Johnny had been in situ as the Republic of Ireland 'manager' for ten years. The word manager is highlighted as still, all those years on, the Ireland squad was picked by a committee, and it was for Johnny and his helpful lieutenants Noel Cantwell and Charlie Hurley, in particular, to then shape them into a competitive side. Some things had improved, as opposed to 1955, travel by air was the norm rather than the old way of the overnight ferry and then only a couple of hours to catch up on Sunday when in Ireland. Even flying though still left precious little time. Away matches were different of course, as you generally had a couple of days to prepare. During those ten years Johnny had managed Blackburn Rovers, Everton, Leyton Orient and now in 1965, Nottingham Forest so was fully aware of any potential Republic of Ireland players performing over in England.

Considering the administrative situation and the relative lack of importance of football in comparison to traditional Irish sports Johnny had achieved a very decent level of performance for Ireland. As comparative minnows in the international scene, they had only just missed a minimum of a play-off in the 1958 World Cup qualifiers against England. In the qualifiers for the 1962 World Cup they had lost out Czechoslovakia, the eventual runners-up of the tournament. In the European Nations Cup, they had lost out to their nemesis Czechoslovakia in 1960 and in 1964 to the eventual winners Spain. Away from the major competitions they also had beaten the then World Cup holders West Germany in a 1956 friendly, and for good measure beat them again in Germany in 1960 and had also beat the 1958 World Cup finalists Sweden. By 1965 though, all thoughts were on the forthcoming 1966 World Cup competition which was to be held just across the Irish Sea in England.

Ireland were given a most interesting qualifying group which had Spain, the current European Nations champions, and Syria. One side to go through to England, but the group was left in difficulties straight away as Syria pulled out of the World Cup leaving just Spain and Ireland to compete. Syria were supporting the African countries over the allocation of their places for the finals, the Africans view was that they should not have to play a play-off to gain entry to the finals.

A friendly at home to Belgium did not help settle pre-tournament nerves as Ireland lost 2-0 in Dublin. Nevertheless, the whole country was firmly behind the team as Spain arrived at Dalymount Park in early May 1965, with 40,772 passionate fans inside the stadium. There was no doubt that the side Johnny had to manage was one of the strongest he had been given. Four of the team had just won the Football League for Manchester United, goalkeeper Pat Dunne, full-backs Tony Dunne and Shay Brennan, and Noel Cantwell playing again at centre-forward. When you added Johnny Giles, by now a marvellous inside forward for Leeds United, and the still outstanding centre-half Charlie Hurley of Sunderland you had an experienced team. They knew full well that a victory of any sort was vital as qualification was still based on points only, so, if the teams were level after the two matches, a play-off would be required.

Spain were a top-class side though and must have felt that a draw in Ireland would be sufficient to secure qualification to the 1966 World Cup Finals in England. They had an early shock though when a Charlie Hurley effort was disallowed. The match was dominated by defences on both sides, although midfielder Johnny Giles, was probably the most influential player on the pitch. Midway through the second-half came the decisive moment when winger Frank O'Neill of Shamrock Rovers, one of only two home-based players in the Ireland side, sent a free kick too near the Spanish goalkeeper Iribar, but under pressure from Noel Cantwell, Iribar deflected the ball into his own net. The Dublin crowd exploded and became a real twelfth man as Ireland held out for another fine victory under Johnny's management, adding the reigning European Nations Champions to the list of his notable scalps.

The return leg was to be played in Seville in October 1965 with a draw giving Ireland the ticket to the 1966 World Cup Finals in nearby England. The Spanish public seemed unsure of their side's chances, as just under 30,000 attended and were even more unsettled when Andy Mc Evoy scored just before the half-hour mark. The match, and the tie really, was then turned on its head just before half-time, when Barcelona's centre-forward Pereda scored two inside three minutes. He completed his hat-trick in the second half, and Spain scored a fourth to give them an emphatic 4-1 victory. The sides though were level on two points each, and a play-off would be necessary.

The venue chosen for the play-off still leaves a sour taste in Irish football fans' memories. Spain wanted Portugal or Spain itself, hardly neutral! Ireland wanted London, Liverpool or Manchester but the venue chosen was to be Paris, which on the face of it seems neutral, but it had a very high exiled Spanish population. Such was the partisanship that Pat Dunne, Ireland and

Manchester United goalkeeper, remarked that the only Irish flag he saw was the one on the flagpole! There were many rumours at the time that the Irish FA had agreed to take Spain's share of the gate split, and even tales of expensive Spanish wine heading Dublin way, whatever the truth, the Irish committee did not seem to have made the prospect of an even playing field their priority.

A more significant blow on the pitch was the loss, due to injury, of centre-half Charlie Hurley. This meant Noel Cantwell had to demonstrate his complete versatility by dropping back into the number five shirt. Shelbourne's Eric Barber had made his debut at number nine for Ireland in the game in Seville and was very impressed on the workload that Noel Cantwell took on for the team, on and off the pitch. *'Noel was really the front man for the players whilst Johnny Carey had the overall responsibility.'*

A crowd of 35,000 turned up for the game in Paris, with as expected, virtually all present supporting Spain. The game though was very similar to the match in Dublin with both sides playing tight defensively, naturally very wary of making that one mistake which would settle the game, and qualification to the 1966 World Cup Finals. With time ticking on, it was a goal from right-winger Ufarte which decided everything with ten minutes to play. Johnny's dream of a World Cup Final was gone...

By 1966 Johnny had the 1968 European Championships (as they were then re-titled) to concentrate on for Ireland with the news that they would be in a group alongside Turkey and, yet again Czechoslovakia and Spain! They would be played later in the year, a year which had seen England crowned as World Champions after their 4-2 extra time victory over West Germany at Wembley Stadium.

Ireland had actually provided West Germany with some pre-tournament practice as they visited Dublin in May 1966. The Irish public showed their frustration at the happenings over the venue of the play-off match with Spain with only 16,000 turning up at Dalymount Park, to see one of the leading teams in world football play against a very inexperienced Ireland team lacking Noel Cantwell, Johnny Giles and Tony Dunne amongst others. Five members of the West Germany side would appear in the World Cup Final two months on and Beckenbauer, Overath and Haller were amongst the scorers as they comfortably beat Ireland 4-0 with the legendary Uwe Seeler captaining the team and class stopper Schulz holding the defence together.

A mini-tour of Europe playing two other nations who would not be appearing at the 1966 World Cup Finals, saw matches in Vienna, Austria where the hosts won a very physical game 1-0, before a trip to Liege, Belgium where only 5,000 were attracted to the game, but where Ireland overturned their home defeat 12 months earlier to record a fine 3-2 victory. These would be the third and fourth internationals Johnny Carey could not actually attend in his management role with Ireland. This time it was due to a tour arranged for his then league side, Nottingham Forest. His two senior players, Noel Cantwell and Charlie Hurley would take over the running of the team in these two fixtures.

By the time the 1968 European Championship qualification matches started, Johnny also realised that, finally, his Nottingham Forest team were going to be a real force in the 1966-67 First Division over in England. The pressures and the responsibility of overseeing two sides, both involved in serious competitions, the First Division with his club side Nottingham Forest and the European Championships with his beloved Republic of Ireland were really growing on Johnny. Before Christmas 1966, Ireland would play both Spain and Turkey in Dublin and also play Spain over in Valencia. The results left qualification in serious doubt...

The Irish players certainly felt that they really owed Spain after the controversy of the 1966 World Cup qualification, but the match followed the lines of the previous time the two countries had met in Dublin, only this time Iribar in the Spanish goal, did not palm the ball into his own net! A 0-0 draw though was still a decent performance, but Ireland needed to win their home ties, and it left them a difficult route to qualification. Three weeks later though, in the first-ever meeting between the Republic of Ireland and Turkey, a match played in Dublin, Ireland registered a 2-1 victory.

Johnny had very high regard for Noel Cantwell and Charlie Hurley, both of whom would be his captains on and off the pitch. Charlie Hurley had been the captain for the match against Turkey, and such was Johnny's regard for him, when the return tie with Spain was played in Valencia in early December 1966, he picked Charlie even though he was having injury problems for his club side Sunderland and was not a regular in their team at the time. Players such as Noel Cantwell, Johnny Giles and Andy McEvoy were all unavailable for the tie in Spain. Despite superb performances by goalkeeper Alan Kelly and Charlie Hurley in defence, Spain eased to a 2-0 victory.

February 1967 was a pivotal month in the football career of Johnny Carey. His Nottingham Forest side lost a potential title-deciding match away at Manchester United 1-0 to a fantastic late Denis Law goal before, on 22 February in Ankara, Turkey, his involvement as one of the Republic of Ireland's greatest ever footballers and long-serving managers finally came to an end.

Johnny had felt for a long time that the Irish committee was never going to relent and give their manager total control. He had now been a player and a manager for 30 years and decided to call it a day as far as Ireland were concerned when qualifications for the 1968 European Championships were sealed. The match against Turkey would also be the last playing international as far as Noel Cantwell was concerned and, sadly for both, Ireland were on the end of a 2-1 defeat. Fittingly, Noel was the only player to have appeared in Johnny's first and last sides, and he did score a late consolation goal. The last side Johnny would lead while Republic of Ireland manager being: Kelly; Kinnear; Finucane; McGrath; Hurley; Meagan; O'Neill; Dunphy; Cantwell; Giles and Gallagher.

During his 12 years as manager, Johnny Carey was involved in 45 internationals, of which 17 were victories, 7 draws and 21 defeats. Considering the lack of real quality in depth amongst his players, and his lack of control over selection, his record was good. If some lacked quality, this was more than made up for by the players who would run their last breath for their manager and their country. His tenure included some excellent victories against the leading football nations between 1955 and 1967 such as West Germany (twice) Czechoslovakia, Sweden, Spain, beating Scotland when they had a star-studded side and only being held by an England side in the last minute, a team which included four of the Busby Babes. Johnny Carey could hold his head high, he had done his country proud.

As a final note to this chapter we will consider the wonderful words of Mick Meagan. Mick played under Johnny at Everton and for Ireland. He would go on to be the first manager of Ireland to have control over team selection. Recalling Johnny, Mick had this to say, *'As children Johnny was one of our idols playing for Manchester United. He was probably the first player my age group would have looked up to, it was always a great thrill when he would come home and play for Ireland. He was very popular as a manager at Everton and it was more or less his side than won the league in 1962. Not only was he a wonderful player but a very, very nice person. Any of the older players that I spoke to about him had great praise for him especially Peter Farrell who played with him for Ireland and said he was a wonderful person, a great player and a credit to his country. When I went to Huddersfield, Henry Cockburn was a coach there, he had played for England and he also played with Carey on the great United team that won the cup. Henry had nothing but great words for Carey. Henry used always say to me, "It doesn't matter how much I coach you I will never make you into a Carey." When Johnny was manager of Everton, I learned he was a very proud Irish man, I was the only Irish player at Everton then. Johnny was always on to me to get another interest other than football, he used to give an example of this young player in Blackburn who after training would go to Wigan market, get a stall and sell bits and pieces. He used to say to me to do the same. That same young lad he spoke about was Dave Whelan who became chairman of Wigan and ended up owning all the JJ sports! So, it's a pity I didn't listen! Another time the Irish team stayed overnight at London Airport Hotel to catch an early flight. We all arrived down for breakfast in our casual gear when Johnny arrived down he ordered us back upstairs to change into our suits. He said we were representing our country and must look respectful. I enjoyed playing for Johnny both for Everton and Ireland.'*

Chapter Fourteen

A ROVER'S RETURN

Johnny Carey started his managerial career in the summer of 1953 at Blackburn Rovers. It would be to Blackburn that he would return after leaving Nottingham Forest in 1969, and it would be there that his glorious career in football would end in the summer of 1971.

They say never go back, and of course, hindsight is a marvellous attribute, but Johnny was asked to return to Blackburn to work alongside his former player, Eddie Quigley, who had taken over as the Rovers manager following Jack Marshall's resignation in 1967. Johnny's role was intended to be as the Blackburn Rovers administrator working alongside Eddie.

In recent times, Blackburn Rovers had seen the end of the playing careers of stalwarts such as Bryan Douglas and Ronnie Clayton, while Mike England and Fred Pickering had left in big transfer moves, so the club had not progressed from the time Johnny left in 1958. They had initially stabilised their first division position, which Johnny had led them to, and reached the final of the FA Cup in 1960 after he had left for Everton. In the cup final they had lost 3-0 to Wolverhampton Wanderers, not helped by the infamous injury sustained by full-back Dave Whelan. In later times, Whelan would become a very successful businessman and lead Wigan Athletic to positions in the football world they could not have imagined. By 1966 though, just as England was celebrating winning the World Cup, Blackburn Rovers fans were having to come to terms with the fact that their time in the First Division was over. Relegation meant it would be Division Two for them again. Indeed, by the end of the 1968-69 season, it very nearly had been the Third Division as Rovers finished in a lowly 19th position.

The club clearly needed a man of experience to steady the ship. Reflecting on Johnny's time as a manager, he had the wisdom and experience to understand what made a football club tick. As the Nottingham Forest chairman Tony Wood mentioned in his fulsome tribute to Johnny when his time at Forest was up, *'I feel he is one of the greatest administrators in the game'* was Tony's comment. It was in that role, perhaps akin to the modern concept of a director of football, that he returned to Blackburn Rovers, with Eddie Quigley continuing to control the football team at the start of the 1969-70 season.

The team had made a promising start to that season and were top of Division Two by Christmas 1969, but Johnny's skills as an administrator were to be tested. A substantial offer for Keith Newton from Everton, the last of 'Carey's Chicks' from back in the 1950's, was received. The offer was accepted. The transfer and a subsequent lack of replacements meant that the second part of the season was mostly downhill.

The Blackburn Rovers supporters assumed that the £80,000 fee for Keith Newton, a significant figure for a defender in those days, would go towards strengthening the side for a promotion push. Johnny though knew in his new role that money had to be treated with real care, and much to the fans' frustration the amount of the transfer that could be spent on strengthening the side was spent by Eddie Quigley on a goalkeeper! When further cost-cutting occurred, with fans' favourites John Coddington and Jimmy Fryatt leaving, together with Adam Blacklaw and 1966 World Cup squad member John Connolly (two players whose best seasons had been over at rivals Burnley), the decline of Blackburn Rovers was there for all to see.

In the first season after Johnny's return, Rovers would finish eighth in the Second Division and suffered a bad home defeat to Swindon Town in the 3rd round of the FA Cup, so it was also on the field, as well as off, that problems mounted. Realising that at least one new face that fans could get behind was needed for the 1970-71 season, Eddie Quigley moved for an up-and-coming midfielder close by at Bury called Jimmy Kerr. Sadly, having missed the first five matches due to a pre-season injury, Jimmy Kerr was then injured so severely it would finish a very promising career.

Shortly after this blow, Rovers lost to local rivals Bolton Wanderers in the League Cup, the Wanderers themselves were fellow strugglers in the Second Division at the time. This prompted the Blackburn Rovers board to ask Eddie Quigley and Johnny to swap positions, hoping that Johnny could reproduce his glory days in charge during the mid-1950's and steer Rovers to safety. The writing was already on the wall, however, and the selling of their only goal-scoring threat, Ken Knighton to Hull City, to be replaced by former favourite Fred Pickering virtually confirmed relegation. Pickering was nowhere near the player that had left Ewood Park for Everton, and by the end of April, with only six victories to their name, Blackburn Rovers, one of the most famous clubs in English football, were relegated to the Third Division for the first time in their illustrious history.

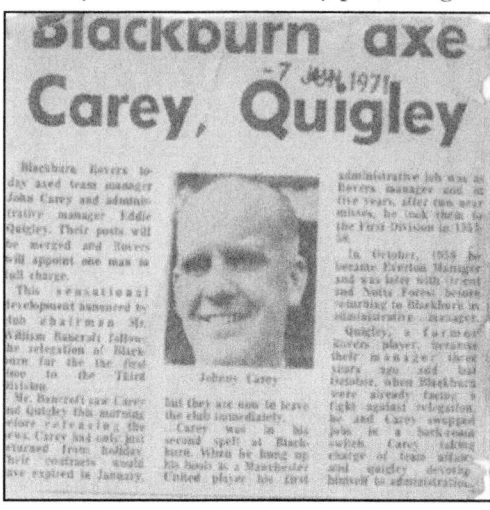

Figure 41 'Blackburn Axe Carey, Quigley'

Even so, it was still seen as a surprising move in early June 1971 when, shortly after returning from a family holiday, Johnny along with Eddie

Quigley were relieved of their duties as the Blackburn Rovers managerial and administrative duo. In his usual calm manner, Johnny accepted his fate. *'It's nothing to worry about, I regard and understand it as part and parcel of the game of football. If your club gets relegated you expect to get the sack, so this decision did not altogether take me by surprise. I cannot really complain, the club have fully honoured my contract until January 1972, although I do feel that time was my real enemy as I only took over the football side of the role in late October'.* With those words, Johnny ended his 18-year long career as a football manager, in which time he had led four club sides (one twice) and his nation.

As with our look at his times at his previous clubs, let his wife Margaret, paint the picture of his recall to Blackburn Rovers. *'When Rovers offered Jack the role as Administrative Manager, working alongside Eddie Quigley, Eddie was the first to ring him and say he was all for it. This role was just what Jack wanted as he had enough of being a team manager and we had been very happy in our first stay in Blackburn. And so, we left Nottingham, leaving yet another child behind, this time Marie. During the second season, the Rovers board asked Jack and Eddie to swop jobs, which they did reluctantly but it was too late to turn the side around, and after a few months the axe fell again. In spite of the ups and downs life has been good to us and we have no regrets. Jack has always done his best, honestly and sincerely, and I still say he is the best manager in England. The real bonus though is that after all the worries, he is going to settle down to a 9 till 5 job which is sheer heaven after all the worries, and yet if the opportunity came again I just can't help wondering...'* The final sentence paints a vivid picture from a perspective that is not usually seen. A life in football is portrayed in terms of success and failure of the team on the pitch. The toll on family life and the sacrifices made are rarely reported.

A NEW LIFE

Johnny's heavenly 9-to-5 job that Margaret Carey refers to was at Trafford Town Hall for Sale Borough Council as it was then, in the very imposing building opposite Lancashire County Cricket Club. He took to his new life very well, enabling him to play golf and see his family when he could, as grandchildren instead of footballers became the weekend interests! In the mid-1970's, the Manchester United manager of the time, Tommy Docherty asked Johnny to do some scouting for the club he still called *'his'* club. Docherty's assistant was Tommy Cavanagh, the man who had been alongside Johnny when he so nearly achieved the double as Nottingham Forest manager.

Margaret Carey raised the question, *'What if the opportunity arose again?'* Might that opportunity have occurred during a time of turbulence at Manchester United from 1969 when, the recently knighted Sir Matt Busby, retired. Would Johnny have provided that stabilising factor, perhaps alongside the young Wilf McGuinness? Or the duo of Johnny Carey and Noel Cantwell by 1970, which would have been an exciting combination.

Although Johnny was never in the Shankly, Revie, Docherty or Clough style of manager, he had all the attributes required of a successful manager. He had experience of playing and leading club sides to a fair level of success and taking his Ireland side as far as could be expected in competitions such as the World Cup and European Championship qualifiers, despite the sparse number of quality players at his disposal. He had an aura about him, calmness and utmost respect, from people who either played alongside him, were managed by him or simply knew of his reputation.

It wasn't to be though, and after Blackburn Rovers for the second time, Johnny and his beloved wife Margaret, settled in Bramhall for over 20 years as recalled in the introduction to this book. After Johnny retired from his time at Sale Borough Council, he and Margaret moved to an apartment in Handforth, before in 1990 at the age of 71, Johnny developed Alzheimer's. Margaret Carey was the rock in Johnny's life, and she dutifully tended him for five years before he passed away at Macclesfield Hospital on the 23 August 1995 aged 76.

Let us end this chapter by hearing Margaret's memories of Johnny's later years. A tribute that no doubt would have given him more satisfaction than all of his football awards: *'The developing of our children and then the joy of grandchildren from them gave Jack and me real happiness. Tragically Jack was stricken with Alzheimer's, but I was able to nurse him until a week before he died in hospital from a chest infection. Three days a week he went into Day Care to give me a break. All the Nurses and Doctors called him 'Gentleman John' which was his nickname in the football world. In spite of his dreadful illness, he remained his gentle self to the end'.*

Chapter 15

GENTLEMAN JOHN

This chapter pays a final tribute to Johnny Carey in the words of those that knew him best. Behind every great man is a great woman they say. Well, as some of these pages will have shown, Margaret Carey was an enormous influence on Johnny Carey's life and footballing career. She would live on for a further 17 years after her beloved Jack's death before she passed away in a Wilmslow Care Home in 2012 at the age of 93.

MICHAEL CAREY

Their eldest son, Michael has been a great help and support to us in the production of this book about his father. Michael, like Margaret, penned thoughts on his time as Johnny Carey's son, on the family, Johnny's all-round sporting interests, his time going to Old Trafford and the final days of his father's life:

Family Man

'Dad was an absolutely wonderful father to his four children- my youngest brother Gerry, my sisters Marie, Pat and me. I know from talking to my mother that he was also a great husband and friend. He had an amazing ability to make everyone feel at ease with him, whoever they were and from whatever background. He was just as comfortable talking to the managing director of a company as to the cleaner. He was extremely modest, and I don't think it occurred to anyone to be envious of him. He had a dry sense of humour and could see the funny side of a situation very easily.

I think he was completely non-judgemental about people and always brought out the best in them, which is an ideal quality for a captain. Having said that, he was a big softy in many ways. Mum and my sister Pat used to tease him sometimes, but he always took it in good part!

For such a prominent sportsman he was fairly quiet in company, not wanting to be the centre of attention. I think he was quite shy as a person, but on the other hand, he was not shy about performing. Obviously, as a footballer, he gave very good speeches at Boys Clubs, schools and swanky hotels. He was always in demand.

He was a Roman Catholic and went to Mass every week of his life, and although he never talked about his religion, I think it was very important to him.

My father was very good with his grandchildren and used to get down on the floor to play with them and teach them some great tricks. He had a special bond with all of them. He was known as Grandy.

My mother was actually the one who did the disciplining in the family, dad was the soft one, although you could always tell he expected a certain standard of behaviour from you and it would never occur to you to let him down.

He was absolutely the best dad in the world, and we all loved him very much'.

An All-Round Sportsman

'Dad loved all sports, not just football. He played golf every Sunday morning and got his handicap down to 4 at one stage. He was a fine tennis player and watched most other sports on the television, I think as a professional sportsman he could appreciate the level of skill and commitment in all disciplines.

He told me a funny story of his time in the army when he was nominated for the boxing team. His opponent was a massive guy and a champion who came out of his corner with all guns blazing and took a mighty swing at dad's head. He ducked in fear, but the guy hit him so hard on the top of dad's head that he broke his thumb! Dad was declared the winner!'

Sunday Mornings at Old Trafford

'In those times, mums and young children did not tend to go to the matches, although dad would take me to the ground on a Sunday morning after Mass. He would just be checking how any injured player was or talking about the game the previous day.

The old player's tunnel was on the halfway line but behind the present tunnel was a large wooden building, which actually resembled a Scout's Hut! This was actually the physio unit run by Tom Curry, who all the players loved. I do recall the overpowering smell of liniment. One day the United reserve goalkeeper came bounding in, jumped up and cracked his head on one of the cross beams, doing a double somersault in the process. As a kid, I thought this very funny!'

Final Times

'Dad died in 1995, and after much thought, my mother decided that she did not want him buried in a cemetery. I think she felt his spiritual home was always Old Trafford, home of Manchester United.

The chairman at the time was Martin Edwards, and he very kindly agreed that we could scatter dad's ashes in the goalmouth at the Stretford End. Looking back, his life was defined by his time at Manchester United, and it was felt to be fitting. So, on the appointed day, we went to the club with the Funeral Director, met up with Martin and made our way down to the pitch.

I recall it looked so big at ground level, it must be amazing to play there. We walked over to the goalmouth, and I scattered the ashes. It was the right thing. Even though the pitch will have been re-laid many times, we will always imagine dad as a giant striding across it during his great career as a Manchester United player there.

His important medals, international shirts and trophies are all housed in the Manchester United Museum for future generations to appreciate.

He was a great man-Gentleman John.'

Over his time in football, from 1936 back in Dublin, until the end of his second time in charge at Blackburn Rovers in 1971, Johnny Carey played with, against and managed some of the game's greatest men. He is, without doubt, a Manchester United and Republic of Ireland legend. Indeed, the first big name Irish footballer, while his days at Blackburn Rovers, Everton, Leyton Orient and Nottingham Forest have left a lifetimes memory.

Here are just a few quotes about Johnny Carey, starting with the man he was inexorably linked with from their times at Manchester United, Sir Matt Busby.

SIR MATT BUSBY

'People who know me will vouch for the fact that I never indulge in idle adulation, but I am certain that Johnny Carey was one of the truly great players of all times. From our first meeting it convinced me that he was something special, more than just a great footballer, his every action suggested that he was a thinker, a student of the game prepared to go to any lengths to achieve his goal-soccer perfection. When I was appointed manager of Manchester United one of my first jobs was to appoint him as club captain, as soon as I had settled in it was obvious that only one man could be the skipper; that man was Johnny Carey. I think time proved what a good decision it was. It is difficult to do honour to a soccer genius through the medium of the written word because the ability that Johnny possessed had to be seen to be appreciated to the full.'.

SIR STANLEY MATTHEWS, perhaps the most famous footballer of his day:

'No mention of the forties and fifties could be complete without including the talents of Johnny Carey. He wasn't known for his pace, but he more than made up for it by an astute and intelligent use of the ball and uncanny sense of positioning. He still had years left when he decided to retire, and the temptation to carry on must have been a strong one. But two considerations weighed heavily on his mind- a reluctance to carry on in the public eye for a day longer than he could guarantee a flawless performance and a concern that to stay longer would deny similar privileges to a youngster coming through the ranks at Old Trafford. Johnny Carey was a truly great footballer.'

FRANK SWIFT, regarded as one of England's great ever goalkeepers, sadly died in the Munich air disaster when fulfilling his reporting duties:

'Johnny Carey was that lovable Irishman to me. He was a great player, I remember one game he played and captained for Ireland against England. He started at right-half although just before kick-off the Irish centre-forward nearly dropped out and Johnny was going to play centre-forward. In the second half he went to left-back when the full-back was injured, and over the whole match he was the best player on the pitch, with such as Tommy Lawton, Tom Finney and Billy Wright in our team.'

BILLY FOULKES, a man who won the European Cup, FA Cup and four League titles for Manchester United:

'Johnny Carey was one of the classiest operators, whether at right-back or right-half that it has been my privilege to see. When I played behind him for the first time, making my senior debut at Liverpool in 1952, he looked an old guy, balding, a bit stooped, shorts too long for him, not the idea of a professional footballer. But he didn't take long to open my eyes, just strolling through the action, intercepting and prompting, always cool and

always in control. He was superb in the air, just flicking balls unerringly to teammates and I left the field thinking how lucky to have played alongside such a master. I learnt so much form just one game, then after the match the captain came up to me and asked my age. I told him I was 20; he looked me in the eye and declared, in that soft Irish brogue of his, "I think you will do well" That's all it was, nothing over the top to turn a young fellows head, but it made me feel eight foot tall.'

WILF McGUINNESS, Busby Babe then manager of Manchester United:
'The United right-back and captain at the start of my career was a soft-spoken Dubliner Johnny Carey, the cream of footballers. He was such a smooth operator who always seemed to have plenty of time, and it seemed nobody could get past him. Even if he was up against a flyer, he just put his body between his opponent and the ball, and he never looked like committing a foul, even if it was. Gentleman John as he was known, just exuded class. He was a stylish, all-round performer.'

GEOFFREY GREEN, revered journalist:
'Here indeed was a man who had been one of the outstanding footballers of his times, an architect of the constructive defence in almost as great a way as Stanley Matthews, the destroyer of defences. At first glance he looked older than he was, but Johnny Carey never encouraged any exploitation of his personality. For him the game was one thing; personal triumphs at best were an irrelevance. If he rightly won his place among the great right-backs, he must rank as the finest all-round footballer who ever took the field.'

BILLY BINGHAM, former player under Johnny Carey at Everton, later manager of Everton & Northern Ireland;
'I noticed that Johnny Carey was cool, calculating, a very shrewd man who would have used those attributes in his wonderful playing career as he did managing players.'

TOMMY DOCHERTY, player at Preston North End and Arsenal, then manager at many clubs including Manchester United and the Scotland national side.
'Johnny Carey could play in six positions with ease anywhere on the park outstandingly well. A magnificent footballer and man.'

JOHN DOHERTY, Manchester United & Leicester City footballer and former Chair of the United Old Players Association:
'Johnny Carey was an amazing footballer, in his own way something of a genius. Whilst this is a strong word, a mere glance at Johnny's career shows it is appropriate. A player who appeared in the United first team in 9 positions including a full game in goal at Sunderland in 1953. Johnny Carey had a superb touch with both his feet, magnificent in the air, and whilst his pace was not the greatest it was never an issue as his shrewdness ensured he got through every time. Nobody, but nobody seemed to have a bad word about him such was his impact on the game of football as a player, manager and man.'

This has been the story of a man who lived his life to the full, honestly, religiously and a complete family man. He happened to be the greatest Irish footballer of his time, as good a player as any in the world, and, without a doubt, a genuine Manchester United and Ireland legend. Throughout his life and career, he was always a gentleman.

JOHNNY CAREY – GENTLEMAN JOHN

CAREER STATISTICS

Before joining Manchester United Johnny Carey played minor football for Home Farm followed by six games as an amateur for St James' Gate in Dublin at the start of the 1936-37 season.

Professional Playing Career

Club Football

Years	Team	App	(Gls)
1937-38	Manchester United	19	(4)
1938-39	Manchester United	34	(6)
1945-46	Manchester United	4	(0)
1946-47	Manchester United	33	(0)
1947-48	Manchester United	43	(1)
1948-49	Manchester United	49	(1)
1949-50	Manchester United	43	(1)
1950-51	Manchester United	43	(0)
1951-52	Manchester United	39	(3)
1952-53	Manchester United	37	(1)
1937–53	**Manchester United**	**304**	**(17)**

Wartime Football

		App	(Gls)
1939-43	Manchester United	112	(49)

Guest appearances for Cardiff City (1), Manchester City (1), Shamrock Rovers (2), Everton (1) & Liverpool (1).

International Football

		App	(Gls)	
1937-53	Ireland (FAI)	29	(3)	
1940	League of Ireland XI	1	(0)	
1946-49	Ireland (IFA)	9	(0)	(Including two 'Victory Internationals')
1947	Europe XI	1	(0)	
1937-53	**Total**	**40**	**(3)**	

Management Career

Club Football

		P	W	D	L	
1953–58	Blackburn Rovers	237	119	50	68	(Promotion to Division One, 1958)
1958–61	Everton	122	51	49	22	
1961–63	Leyton Orient	100	35	24	41	(Promotion to Division One, 1962)
1963–68	Nottingham Forest	254	97	63	93	
1970–71	Blackburn Rovers	38	5	13	20	
1953-71	**Total**	**751**	**307**	**199**	**244**	

International Football

		P	W	D	L
1955-67	Republic of Ireland	45	17	7	21

Over a professional career spanning 1937-71 Johnny Carey played or managed a total of 1258 games.

LIST OF FIGURES

Figure 1 Young Johnny.. 5
Figure 2 Goalkeeper Billy Behan 8
Figure 3 Black-haired Irishman. 9
Figure 4 The happy couple! 14
Figure 5 The devastated main stand.. 16
Figure 6 Manchester Guardian Headline, 2 September 1946...................................... 22
Figure 7 Match report of a classic game... 30
Figure 8 'Those far away places' 31
Figure 9 Leading the team out... 36
Figure 10 Proudly holding the cup. 37
Figure 11 Johnny the builder 38
Figure 12 Playing record of United's '48' side.. 39
Figure 13 'Arsenal Three Up' 43
Figure 14 Threat to Irish Players (Aberdeen Press).. 46
Figure 15 Footballer of the Year 47
Figure 16 'Welcome Home!' 50
Figure 17 United on Tour in the USA (1952).. 56
Figure 18 The birth of the "Babes" 61
Figure 19 Manchester Evening Chronicle 64
Figure 20 A magnificent cake!.. 66
Figure 21 United Review - Charity Shield.. 67
Figure 22 What a line-up!... 69
Figure 23 Boro escape the drop. 75
Figure 24 Johnny at his desk.. 79
Figure 25 'The Carey Cult' 83
Figure 26 Blackburn Rovers 1958-59 86
Figure 27 'Carry on Everton' 89
Figure 28 John Moores' message to the Everton faithful 92
Figure 29 A sad farewell 94
Figure 30 The come-back 97
Figure 31 Malcolm Graham celebrates promotion 100
Figure 32 Match Programme, Orient v United 101
Figure 33 New Forest Manager 104
Figure 34 'United unable to cope' 107
Figure 35 Johnny with his pipe 108
Figure 36 Line-ups, Manchester United v Nottingham Forest 109
Figure 37 Johnny surveys the damage.. 114
Figure 38 Liam 'Billy' Whelan.. 119
Figure 39 'Eire were just foiled' 121
Figure 40 Match Programme, Ireland v Scotland 125
Figure 41 'Blackburn Axe Carey, Quigley' 135

ABOUT THE AUTHORS

ROY CAVANAGH MBE
Born in Salford, Roy first saw Manchester United play in 1954. He has contributed to the club programme for six seasons during the 1980's and has had various books on the club and its players published, to date, 20 books including some on Lancashire County Cricket Club. Roy is also an accomplished after dinner speaker and compere. He is married to Barbara, they have two sons, Duncan and Martin, three grandchildren, Claire, Sam and Evie and four great grandchildren, Aila, Harvey, Phoebe and Alice.

CARL ABBOTT
Carl Abbott was formerly Professor of Construction Innovation at the University of Salford. Carl is lucky enough to have been born into a family that is Manchester United through and through. His grandfather, Lawrence, was a steward and season ticket holder as were his father, Roy, and aunt, Ann. So too are his three brothers Roy, Mark and John. His first games were as a young boy in the early 70s, and he has had the honour of following United home and away both domestically and in Europe since that time.

Printed in Great Britain
by Amazon